"In the early 1980s, I was invited to teach summer school at the Notre Dame Catechetical Institute in Middleburg, Virginia. It was there that I first encountered Msgr. Eugene Kevane. Over breakfast, I had the opportunity to benefit from his wisdom and experience as a faithful priest, a sound philosopher and theologian, and a true pedagogue.

Returning after all these years to his book, *The Lord of History*, I felt as though I were renewing those early morning conversations with Msgr. Kevane. With erudition and insight, he moves us beyond the ideological compartmentalization of history, under which we've labored so long, and presents to us instead an authentic philosophy of history which, at its root, is open both to the doctrine of creation and the *mysterium*, the saving plan of the Father, revealed and accomplished by the Pasch of the Incarnate Logos through the Holy Spirit in the very heart of human history. Thus do we glimpse the Lord of History! In setting forth this vision and understanding, Msgr. Kevane offers perennially wise guidance for the intellectual formation of seminarians, priests, and indeed all who engage in the ministry of evangelization and catechesis. After forty years, this volume continues to merit our study and attention."

MOST REVEREND WILLIAM E. LORI
Archbishop of Baltimore, Maryland

"As I worked on my Master's degree under Msgr. Eugene Kevane, he quoted St. Paul in every class: 'O Timothy, guard the deposit of faith' (1 Tim 6:20). He demonstrated his deep desire to do so by astute intellectual reflection as well as total and loving fidelity to the Church's Magisterium. Now, after so many years, his work has become easily available to all those who love the Lord and his Church! It is with great personal joy that I recommend this book."

SR. M. JOHANNA PARUCH, FSGM, PH.D.
Professor of Theology and Catechetics
Franciscan University of Steubenville

"When I wrote the course of studies for Franciscan University's catechetics program, I considered Msgr. Kevane my mentor. His understanding formed my own approach. In this work, Msgr. Kevane presents to priests and catechists the absolutely necessary philosophy of history that 'reveals the mystery of Christ which affects the whole course of human history.' He brings out the revelation of the mystery of Christocentrism and the need for us to pass that on. The kerygma, contained in the Apostles' Creed, must be presented as transforming history. The kerygma is the definite plan for the revelation of God. This plan has two comings: the coming of the Incarnate Word and the Second Coming in glory. This rootedness in time, between the two comings, has had a tendency to disappear in catechesis. It must be brought back.

In *Sapientia Christiana* (1979), Pope St. John Paul II gives the norms for the presentation of the faith. Kevane's book, following in 1980, is an application of the Saint's instruction, still pertinent today. We must go back to a revealed understanding of the world. This book will help take you there."

BARBARA MORGAN
Founding Director of the Office of Catechetics and Former Professor of Catechetics at Franciscan University of Steubenville, Author of Echoing the Mystery, *and Director of Religious Education, Christ the King Catholic Church, Ann Arbor, MI*

BIBLICAL CATECHESIS SERIES
Series Editor: Scott Hahn

Christ commissioned His disciples to go to the ends of the earth and proclaim the Gospel until the close of the age. They were to do this not only in Aramaic or in Greek, but in the language and terms of their time. The Apostles and the great Fathers accomplished this to a remarkable degree. They converted the West through their catechesis.

The essential catechetical mission is to proclaim and promote the faith in contemporary society. To do that effectively, the Catholic tradition—exemplified by the great bishop-mystagogue St. Augustine—brings all disciplines to the aid of theology. The Biblical Catechesis series consists of works by the late Msgr. Eugene Kevane, a disciple and imitator of St. Augustine. These writings deserve to be studied and imitated in their turn by future generations of catechists.

THE
LORD
OF
HISTORY

BIBLICAL CATECHESIS SERIES

THE
LORD
OF
HISTORY

Christocentrism and the
Philosophy of History

EUGENE KEVANE
Foreword by SCOTT HAHN

EMMAUS
ROAD
PUBLISHING
Steubenville, Ohio
www.emmausroad.org

Emmaus Road Publishing
1468 Parkview Circle
Steubenville, Ohio 43952

Library of Congress Cataloging in Publication Data
Names: Kevane, Eugene, author.
Title: The Lord of history : Christocentrism and the philosophy of history /
  Eugene Kevane.
Description: Steubenville : Emmaus Road, 2018. | Originally published:
  Boston, MA : Daughters of St. Paul, 1980. | Includes index.
Identifiers: LCCN 2018017256| ISBN 9781947792869 (hc) | ISBN 9781947792876
  (pb) | ISBN 9781947792883 (eb)
Subjects: LCSH: History--Religious aspects--Christianity--History of
  doctrines. | History--Philosophy--History. | Jesus Christ--Person and
  offices.
Classification: LCC BR115.H5 K48 2018 | DDC 261.5--dc23 LC record available at
  https://lccn.loc.gov/2018017256

NIHIL OBSTAT
Rev. Richard V. Lawlor, S.J.
IMPRIMATUR
+ Humberto Cardinal Medeiros
Archbishop of Boston

Cover image: *Salvator Mundi* (ca. 1750–75) by an unknown Flemish painter,
Museum of Fine Arts, Houston, Texas

Cover design and layout by Margaret Ryland

To St. Thérèse of Lisieux
Apostle of the First Article of the Creed for the Twentieth Century

Contents

FOREWORD

IT was Eugene Kevane's misfortune, some would say, to live in an ideological age, an anti-intellectual age, a time of sloganeering in places
once dedicated to scholarship. It was his misfortune, they would add, to
hold a high position in the administration of a great university, just as
the university was falling into chaos through the rejection of its mission.
The seeming misfortunes abound.

As a philosopher of history, however, Monsignor Kevane knew that
there is no such thing as fortune, and so there is no misfortune. There
is only God's providential design worked out through—and in spite
of—human decisions freely made. "Since the Creator is infinitely intelligent," he once wrote, "philosophical reason by itself can (and should)
recognize that He will have a plan in mind when creating. In carrying
out such a plan God is already the Lord of history."

Because God is Lord of history, he is Lord of each of our personal
lives. Thus, if a man like Eugene Kevane suffers defamation and professional ruin, it is not misfortune, and it need not be a tragedy. These
happen to prove him as a hero. The only tragedy is to fail to be a saint.

• • • • • • •

Eugene Kevane (1913–1996) was and remains the greatest philosopher
I have ever known. He was a prodigy in his mastery of several academic
disciplines: philosophy, theology, history, biblical studies, patrology,
classics, and education. He was visionary in his synthesis. He engaged
intellectual problems in their deepest complexity; yet he wrote with

utter clarity and simplicity. His pages *teach* and never obscure. He had no use for the modern tendency to invent ever-more-specialized technical vocabularies.

I am not alone in holding Monsignor Kevane in high esteem. He was invited to Rome by Cardinal Joseph Ratzinger to mark the centennial celebration of the theologian M. J. Scheeben. He was the first American chosen by Pope John Paul II as a member of the elite Pontifical Roman Theological Academy.

His origins, however, were unlikely for a philosopher. He was born in 1913 on a farm in Buena Vista County, Iowa. He received his early education in a one-room schoolhouse. Later he would study at the Pontifical Gregorian University in Rome and receive advanced degrees from Creighton University and Catholic University of America. He was ordained a priest for the Diocese of Sioux City, Iowa, in 1937.

His passion was pedagogy. He loved Catholic education in general and religious education in particular. He served as a classroom teacher and a principal. He founded a high school, which is still in operation. He joined the education faculty at the Catholic University of America in Washington, D.C., and soon became its most popular teacher. In the heyday of U.S. Catholic schooling, he was promoted to dean of CUA's School of Education.

He was, however, something greater than an educator, greater than an administrator, greater than a philosopher or theologian. And what is that? He was a catechist.

That may seem anticlimactic to readers in the twenty-first century—but that is our fault. We have come to think of catechists as amateurs. We've come to think of "master catechists" as those who have had the time and stamina to undergo diocesan accreditation workshops.

But for me the word evokes the great instructors of the ancient Church: Clement of Alexandria, for example, and the great bishop-mystagogues Cyril of Jerusalem, Ambrose of Milan, John Chrysostom, and Monsignor Kevane's own chosen master, Augustine of Hippo.

Eugene Kevane was a catechist in that tradition—a tradition in which the generalist comes to surpass the specialists in many seemingly disparate fields. And now he had come to occupy what was arguably the most prestigious catechetical position in the United States.

What better place and what better work could there be for a man with his gifts?

The story of what happened next is well told by Peter Mitchell in his history *The Coup at Catholic University: The 1968 Revolution in*

American Catholic Education. In 1967 a group of U.S. Catholic university leaders met in Land O'Lakes, Wisconsin, and drafted a statement that asserted their schools' autonomy from the authority of the bishops. The cause found champions at Catholic University, especially in the School of Theology, where faculty favored a tolerance of active dissent from the Church's established teachings. What they could *not* tolerate, however, was any dissent from their own claims—any challenge to their own sudden and self-declared magisterium.

Monsignor Kevane tried to engage his colleagues in a calm and reasonable dialogue. He argued that their novel claim was inconsistent with the mission of a pontifical university—and, indeed, rendered that mission incoherent.

It was, alas, not a season for conversation. Their response to Dean Kevane's arguments was to demand his dismissal, which they won in January 1968. He was the exemplary victim at the beginning of a reign of terror at the university. Months later, in the wake of the papal encyclical *Humanae Vitae*, faculty knew that they must obey their dissenting overseers or suffer the same fate as Eugene Kevane. No less a theologian than William May confessed, much later, that he signed the protest against *Humanae Vitae* in order to keep his job.

From that time forward, Monsignor Kevane led a peripatetic scholarly life, teaching at a number of institutions—and influencing no small number of rising theologians, those who recognized a one-in-a-generation genius when they met him.

He founded the Notre Dame Catechetical Institute in the Diocese of Arlington, Virginia, which offered the graduate study in catechetics that, in the wake of Land O'Lakes, was no longer available from the major universities.

The students there received a rich education from a master teacher. Monsignor Kevane was interdisciplinary before it was fashionable. Grounded in Augustinian principles, he was nonetheless modern in his concerns, addressing philosophy's subjective turn, theology's historical consciousness, and so on.

Relieved of administrative responsibilities, he found time to write, and he was prolific in his output. He wrote nine books and published frequently in French, German, and Italian scholarly journals, since he was a pariah in Catholic academia in his homeland.

His work was everywhere marked by a quality he attributed to Saint Augustine of Hippo. He called it "The Catholic Fact"—yes, he capitalized each word—and he defined it as "the historical reality of the

Church as a sudden illumination visible in the whole world, *in toto orbe terrarum*." Nowhere did he present his vision so compellingly and completely as in *The Lord of History*.

History, he argues here, takes shape for us only in light of Jesus Christ. That is true of world history as well as Church history. But that is not all. Monsignor Kevane believed that our personal histories—my life, your life, and the lives of our students—make sense only with Christ at the center.

He believed, moreover, that our historical moment was a time of singular grace, when the Holy Spirit was moving the Magisterium of the Church to draw synthetically from the Scriptures, the Fathers, the medieval schoolmen, and especially Saint Thomas Aquinas. The message was rich, but the world was not receiving the message. The abundant harvest was locked away in storehouses, while the people meanwhile went hungry. He saw clearly that he had come to the kingdom for a time such as this.

• • • • • • •

I discovered Monsignor Kevane's work when I was still a Protestant. As I read his high school textbooks, I envied Catholic teenagers the rigor of their intellectual formation. (I didn't know at the time how few schools dared to use these masterpieces of catechesis.) As I drew closer to the Catholic faith, I read everything of his I could lay my hands on. It wasn't easy, in those days before the World Wide Web, to track down his work, appearing as it did from obscure publishers and in overseas periodicals.

I am pleased, now, that I can help bring these books to a wider audience in a new generation. If I believed in fortune, I would call these readers fortunate. I know, however, that they're blessed.

—Scott Hahn

INTRODUCTION

THE *General Catechetical Directory* is lucid and categorical about the first principle of method in religious education. Paragraph number forty states: "Jesus Christ, the incarnate Word of God, since He is the supreme reason why God intervenes in the world and manifests Himself to men, is the center of the Gospel message within salvation history.... Hence catechesis must necessarily be Christocentric."

But if Christ is no longer the center how can a catechist be Christocentric in teaching? If He is no longer the center of the universal history of mankind, how can He be the center of each one's personal history? Is not the very profession of the Apostolic Faith in the Lordship of Jesus at stake?

The Second Vatican Council addresses such questions in one of its most far-reaching statements of position, made, significantly enough, in its *Decree on the Training of Priests*. Pointedly enough as well, granted the agitation among priests and bishops on the right way to renew and update philosophy and theology. That such an agitation exists is a commonplace since Fathers Loisy and Tyrrell early in the present century and a reality since Fathers George Hermes and Anton Günther in the German Universities of mid-nineteenth century. Indeed, the First Vatican Council was called primarily to settle this matter, and the program of *Aeterni Patris* for the renewal of Christian philosophy was intended to be the instrument for effecting this conciliar settlement throughout all the institutions of Catholic higher education.

"In the revision of ecclesiastical studies," states the Second Vatican Council, "the main object to be kept in mind is a more effective coordination of philosophy and theology so that they supplement one another in revealing to the minds of the students with ever increasing clarity the Mystery of Christ, which affects the whole course of human history, exercises unceasing influence on the Church, and operates mainly through the ministry of the priest."[1]

Before an entity can be coordinated with something else, it must continue to exist in its own right. The Council intends, therefore, that philosophy not fall by the wayside or merge somehow into theology. It must continue to be taught in programs of ecclesiastical studies. Vatican II takes it for granted that philosophy will continue to be taught in its own right as an independent intellectual discipline with its own proper object and its own distinctive methodology. Hence it is to have a suitable portion of academic time. When ecclesiastical students, whether seminarians or catechists, receive relatively too little philosophy, even quantitatively, the mind of Vatican II will not be implemented and the renewal of the Church, which it intended, will not be achieved.[2]

When once philosophy has its rightful quantitative presence in terms of the academic time devoted to it, the inevitable qualitative question arises. What kind of philosophy? The issues that depend upon the answer are immense. The very renewal of the Church is at stake.

---

[1] Paul VI, Decree on the Training of Priests *Optatam totius*, October 28, 1965, §14, in Austin Flannery, O.P., ed., *Vatican Council II: The Conciliar and Post Conciliar Documents* (New York: Costello, 1975), 717–718. The official Latin of this passage reads: *In ecclesiasticis studiis recognoscendis eo imprimis spectandum est ut disciplinae philosophicae et theologicae aptius componantur et concordi ratione conspirent ad alumnorum mentibus magis magisque aperiendum Mysterium Christi quad totam generis humani historiam afficit, in Ecclesiam iugiter influit et ministerio sacerdotali praecipue operatur* (AAS 58 [1966], 722). On the decree *Optatam totius*, see The Sacred Congregation for Catholic Education, *Ratio fundamentalis institutionis sacerdotalis: Basic Norms for Priestly Formation* (Rome: Vatican Press, 1970), esp. 55–57, "Studies in Philosophy and Kindred Subjects." For a general study of *Optatam totius,* somewhat marred by the shallowness of its time, see A. Laplante, *La formation des prêtres: Genèse et commentaire du decret conciliare Optatam totius* (Paris: Lethellieux, 1969).

[2] See the introduction to *Optatam totius* in Flannery, 707: "The Council is fully aware that the desired renewal of the whole Church depends in great part upon a priestly ministry animated by the spirit of Christ and it solemnly affirms the critical importance of priestly training." *Mutatis mutandis,* the desired "more effective coordination of philosophy and theology" should take place also in the training and formation of all who assist the priestly ministry, especially catechists who undertake "The Ministry of the Word," the title of Part Two of the *General Catechetical Directory* (Washington, DC: USCC, 1971), nos. 14–35. This is particularly the case in the "Higher Institutes for Training in Pastoral Catechetics," described in no. 109.

The Second Vatican Council is very clear. It must be that kind of philosophy which coordinates with theology, supplements theology, and, in some way to be determined, is in turn supplemented by theology. The purpose is likewise explicitly stated: when philosophy functions in this qualitative mode, it will join theology, while remaining itself, in "revealing the Mystery of Christ . . ."

This position of Vatican II calls for careful analysis. The purpose of the present study is to gather the elements which help to implement this revision of ecclesiastical studies and to indicate some implications for the religious way of thinking proper to the present times of the Church.[3] This will be done in terms of the philosophy of history, that branch of philosophy which has achieved centrality of position in these two hundred contemporary years since Voltaire, Hegel, and Marx. The Council itself points in this direction, for it has in mind a philosophizing, valid as philosophy, which helps "to reveal the Mystery of Christ which affects the whole course of human history."

This implies a certain idea of philosophy, one which completes and fulfills the renewal in philosophy which the Church has sponsored in her own universities, seminaries, and schools since the First Vatican Council.[4]

---

[3] See the *General Catechetical Directory,* no. 88, on "Intellectual Demands" in the catechesis of adolescents: "The adolescent . . . is learning how the intellect is to be used rightly. . . . If catechesis is to be able to awaken an experience of the life of faith, it simply cannot neglect the formation of a religious way of thinking." And the *Directory* adds, within its text: "Cf. First Vatican Council, Constitution *Dei Filius,* Chapter IV." It would be difficult to indicate more plainly that the Catholic Church considers Vatican I and Vatican II to be in full harmony, rather than in the opposition sometimes imagined in the years after Vatican II. The *Directory* concludes: "The intellectual building up of the faith of adolescents must by no means be considered as merely a kind of addition, but rather it should be counted as an essential need for the life of faith. The manner of teaching is of special importance. The catechist, in dialogue with the adolescent, must stimulate the mind of the adolescent." Catechesis, in other words, has its own kind of intrinsic dependence upon *Aeterni Patris* and the renewal of Christian philosophy.

[4] See Leo XIII, "*Aeterni Patris*: Epistola Encyclica de Philosophia Christiana ad mentem sancti Thomae Aquinatis Doctoris Angelici in scholis Catholicis instauranda," in *Acta* (Rome: Ex Typographia Vaticana, 1881); 1:255–284. For the English, cf. Etienne Gilson, ed., *The Church Speaks to the Modern World* (New York: Doubleday Image Books, 1954), 31–54. The encyclical *Aeterni Patris* is dated August 4, 1879. In 1902, Leo XIII published a review of his many years as the Successor of St. Peter in which he himself listed *Aeterni Patris* first among "the principal acts of Our pontificate" (cf. Gilson, 333).

In line with the pastoral nature of the Second Vatican Council, this renewal of philosophy turns from an emphasis on the possibility of saving Christian culture to a saving of the very substance of the Catholic Faith itself, in its very formulation, and in the right understanding and interpretation of its formulas. The renewal, to put it another way, turns to some extent from the academic toward a greater emphasis on the pastoral and the catechetical.[5] These are large issues and perspectives, ones which imply for the philosophy of history that new importance and function for which Vatican II calls.

The basic text of this work was first published as a monograph in *Doctor Communis*, the organ of the Pontifical Academy of St. Thomas founded in Rome by Pope Leo XIII: (1977), pp. 219–249; pp. 378–409; and (1978), pp. 29–51.

The writer wishes to thank Msgr. Antonio Piolanti, Vice President of the Academy and Editor of *Doctor Communis*, for permission to publish it in this form.

August 4, 1979
Eugene Kevane
Centenary of *Aeterni Patris*

---

[5] This shift in perspective, which has become quite visible at the centenary of *Aeterni Patris*, seems destined to be the coming hallmark of the renewal of Christian philosophy as this program of the teaching Church turns into its second century. This point will be discussed further in the Epilogue.

Abbreviations

PL   Patralogia Latina Jacques Paul Migne. Patrologiae Cursus
           Completus. Series Latina.

AAS   Actae Apostolica Sedis

CCL   Corpus Christianorum. Series Latina

1

History and Philosophy in the Classical Culture

THE capacity for history is a mark of the human. History begins as each human being's own personal history. Each carries a personal memory of his own past. The beginning of it is shrouded in each case, for each must learn of it by believing the word of his parents. The end of it is likewise shrouded, although each knows that the end is certain. This memory of personal events and affairs, of one's own *resgestae*, is an elemental human fact. Linked with it is a second capacity, that of thinking reflectively upon the meaning of these events in order to interpret their significance. This capacity for philosophy and hence for a philosophy of history is likewise a mark of the human. History, philosophy, and the philosophy of history begin with the fact of human persons, qualitatively distinct as forms of life on this planet.

Each human family maintains some rudimentary kind of group memory, preserved in oral discourse. This family history is vivid back to the grandparents, fades rapidly with the great-grandparents, and usually disappears beyond them: when families coalesce into the larger groups— the tribes, tongues, peoples, and nations of the earthly scene—group memory of the past continues to set the human apart from the other animal species and kingdoms. Always men hand on a narrative of great events, divine events which took place *in illo tempore,* events which give the tribe its characteristic heritage of beliefs and values, the substance of its education and the meaning of the rites by which its youth passes into

responsible adulthood. And thus man in his early simple tribal condition lived forward in time.[1]

Growth as well as succession in time: great events, immense suf-
ferings in common, victories and defeats, powerful leaders, influential
teachers: *tantae molis erat,* Virgil knew, *Romanam condere gentem.*
Gradually the long prehistory ends, and the earliest civilizations stand
revealed in the light of historical records which survive to the present.
These records are food for thought. "Many peoples have had folk mem-
ories," writes Professor Starr of the University of Illinois, "but only
three seem independently to have evolved the concept of formal written
history. One of these is the Chinese; the second is the Hebrew; the third
. . . is the Greek. The idea of explaining man's present condition by a disciplined, factual description of his past is one of the great achievements
which we owe to Hellenic creativeness."[2]

---

[1]   See Mircea Eliade, *Cosmos and History* (New York: Harper Torchbooks, 1959);
Herbert Kuhn, "The Problem of Primitive Monotheism," in Cecily Hastings and
Donald Nicholl, eds., *Selection II* (London: Sheed and Ward, 1954), 63–86; and
Wilhelm Koppers, *Primitive Man and His World Picture* (London: Sheed and Ward,
1952). Much careful research is needed on the part of younger, postmodern scholars
(to anticipate a point to be made below) to break through the imposition of "modern"
philosophical patterns upon the findings of the sciences, not least the sciences of prehistory. "Twenty years ago," Koppers writes,

> it was still possible to publish a pamphlet with the title, *How God Was
> Created*—by man, it goes without saying. Today, however, the most primitive
> races of the earth raise up their voices, as it were, crying in unanimous protest:
> "You are on a wrong track. Your mental experiments (or rather hypotheses)
> won't work. The belief in a Father God, handed down by our forebears from
> time immemorial, cannot possibly be regarded as a final stage in human devel-
> opment. He must rather be the starting point, as is shown in our creation
> myths. Is this not also the teaching [of] your Bible?" (180)

Cf. William F. Albright, *From the Stone Age to Christianity: Monotheism and the Historical Process* (New York: Doubleday Anchor Books, 1957), and esp. 168–178, "The
Nature and Evolution of Primitive Religion": "There can no longer be any doubt that
Fr. Schmidt has successfully disproved the simple evolutionary progression first set up
by the positivist Comte, fetishism-polytheism-monotheism, or Tylor's animism-pol-
ytheism-monotheism" (171). This is an instance of the postmodern situation in
empirical science, to be discussed further below. For a short but penetrating article on
this question, see Franz Cardinal König, "Does Scientific Atheism Exist?" in *L'Osservatore Romano* English Edition (April 7, 1977), 8–9.

[2]   Chester G. Starr, *The Awakening of the Greek Historical Spirit* (New York: Knopf,
1968), 3. For the background of the emergence of *historia* as an intellectual discipline,
see his Chapter 1, "The World of Epic and Myth," with its discussion of Homer and
History.

Homer still stood in the original tradition of *enarratio,* a recounting of the great events and personalities *in illo tempore* which provide the models and paradigms for the formation of the Greek human being.[3]

HISTORY AS AN INTELLECTUAL DISCIPLINE

With Herodotus something else begins, hence his common recognition as "The Father of History." It is a disciplined and factual description, even somewhat documented, of a segment of the more recent human past. Thucydides develops the idea, and it passes to the Romans. "What mind," asks Polybius in the introduction to his *History of Rome,*

> however commonplace or indifferent, could feel no curiosity to learn the process by which almost the whole world fell under the undisputed ascendency of Rome within a period of less than fifty-three years, or to acquaint itself with the political organ- ization to which this triumph—a phenomenon unprecedented in the annals of mankind—was due? What mind, however infat- uated with other spectacles and other studies, could find a field

---

[3] For the early Mesopotamian annals and chronicles, see James B. Pritchard, ed., *Ancient Near Eastern Texts Relating to the Old Testament* (Princeton, NJ: Princeton University Press, 1950), esp. Part III, "Historical Texts," 227–322. For an insight into the religious character of early historical records. See "The Rituals and the Annals" in the classic work of Fustel de Coulanges, *The Ancient City: A Study on the Religion, Laws and Institutions of Greece and Rome* (New York: Doubleday Anchor Books, 1956), 167–173. "In the minds of the people," he writes,

> all that was ancient was venerable and sacred. . . . Thus history had for the ancients a greater importance than it has for us. It existed a long time before Herodotus and Thucydides, written or unwritten; as simple oral traditions, or in books, it was contemporary with the birth of cities. . . . History com- menced, indeed, with the act of foundation, and recorded the sacred name of the founder. It was continued with the legend of the gods of the city, its pro- tecting heroes. It taught the date, the origin and the reason of every worship, and explained its obscure rites. . . . All this was written for the instruction and the piety of the descendants. . . . These city annals . . . were not a work of art, but a religious work. Later came the writers, the narrators, like Herodotus; the thinkers, like Thucydides. History then left the hands of the priests and became something quite different. (170–171)

Among the Hebrews this original religious character of the official historical records was maintained without change, and stands to this day in the Bible.

of knowledge more profitable than this? . . . The coincidence by
which all the transactions of the world have been oriented in a
single direction and guided towards a single goal is the extraordinary characteristic of the present age. . . . The unity of events
imposes upon the historian a similar unity of composition in
depicting for his readers the operation of the laws of Fortune
upon the grand scale.[4]

This "profitable field of knowledge" is the human discipline invented by
the Greeks and Romans. They called it History, and we of the affiliated
West follow them to this day. It was never a separate "Art" on the cycle
of liberal studies. It was taught and learned as a part of the two comprehensive *artes* of human discourse: Grammar and Rhetoric. Polybius
expresses well history's concept of self-contained meaning, its "philosophy of history," if one will, although the Ancients did not use this
phrase. This meaning was the goal it saw for human history, the empires,
great political, social, cultural, and linguistic entities which proceeded
in succession across the face of antiquity, Babylon, Persia, Alexander
and Greek Hellenism, and the culmination in the Roman Empire. Culmination: for the Roman historians shared the common belief which
Virgil voiced: *imperium sine fine dedi,* a concept which was destined in
thought-provoking fashion to survive the "Fall of Rome" as the *Romidee*
of the Middle Ages.[5]

---

[4] Polybius, *World History* bk. 1, chap. 1–4; in Arnold J. Toynbee, ed., *Greek Historical
Thought from Homer to the Age of Heraclitus* (London: Dent, 1924), 23–24, 26. For
the origin and nature of the concept of "history," see Friedrich Büchsel, "Historeo, Historia," in Gerhard Kittel and Gerhard Friedrich, eds., Geoffrey W. Bromiley, trans.,
Theological Dictionary of the New Testament (Grand Rapids, MI: Eerdmans, 1965),
3:391–396. Translations of the Greek and Latin historians are available in the *Loeb
Classical Library.*

[5] See William M. Green, *Augustine on the Teaching of History* (Los Angeles: University
of California Press, 1944); James Bryce, "Theory of the Medieval Empire," in *The Holy
Roman Empire* (New York: Macmillan, 1904, 1913) 89–120; and "Fall of the Empire,"
ibid., 408–417. Bryce dates it on August 6, 1806, when Napoleon deposed Francis
II, the last Holy Roman Emperor of the Germanic Nation. Cf. the French historian,
Henri Berr, in his Preface to a new edition of F. Lot's classic, *The End of the Ancient
World and the Beginnings of the Middle Ages* (New York: Barnes and Noble, 1953), xv:
"This Roman Empire, whose prestige had fascinated the Barbarians, persists as an ideal
framework, and only disappears in 1806 . . ." This fact which the historians perceive
needs to be correlated with the Hebrew Fact, the Catholic Fact, the conversion of the
Fourth Empire, Christendom, and the Great Apostasy of the Nations, matters to be
considered below as given by history to philosophical reflection and analysis. On the

This is some sort of understanding, indeed, of meaning and direction in human affairs, of linear movement toward a goal. But it does not come from philosophy in any formal sense: it is not the result of the application of philosophy to what is taken as given in history. Hence it is not a "philosophy of history" in the modern sense of the phrase since Voltaire and Hegel.

Herodotus retains some vestiges of openness to reports of factual and therefore "historical" interventions from a higher order of reality beyond this visible cosmos, but after him the classical historians in general present their narratives as a purely human, this-worldly panorama of causes and effects in the order of phenomena. This secularized condition left no place for historical intervention by Someone who could qualify as the Lord of history, holding its course and destiny in His hands by virtue of His creation of all the entities that are actors on its stage and which figure in its panorama.

The *technai*, or liberal arts, which constituted the curriculum of the *paideia,* the Greek educational system, were organized upon two different patterns throughout classical antiquity.[6] In one, Rhetoric was the culminating discipline, with its inclusion of history within itself, and with its exclusive concern with successful practical life in this world. In the other pattern, Rhetoric was moved to a lower position to provide room for a new seventh art, culminating the formation of the Greek citizen. It was the discipline called philosophy, and this place as the seventh of the seven liberal disciplines, understanding seven as a symbolic number meaning all the components of a curriculum, was maintained from Socrates, Plato, and Aristotle to its victory over the other pattern in the emergence of Christian philosophy with Augus-

---

idea of Rome, pagan and Christian, see Eric Voegelin, "The Struggle for Representation in the Roman Empire" in *The New Science of Politics: An Introduction* (Chicago: The University of Chicago Press, 1952), 76–106.

[6] See the Introduction in Han Friedrich August von Arnim, *Leben und Werke des Dio von Prusa, Mit einer Einleitung: Sophistik, Rhetorik, Philosophie in ihrem Kampf um die Jugendbildung* (Berlin: Weidmannsche Buchhandlung, 1898), 1–114; for a short study from Augustine's point of view, based on von Arnim, see E. Kevane, "Augustine and Isocrates," *The American Ecclesiastical Review* (November, 1963): 301–321. The breakthrough by philosophy to a reality higher than the cosmic order of the Archaic Culture is a basic theme of Voegelin's work, and especially pp. 52–75: "Through the opening of the soul the philosopher finds himself in a new relation with God; he not only discovers his own psyche as the instrument for experiencing transcendence, but at the same time discovers the divinity in its radically nonhuman transcendence" (67).

tine and the Fathers of the Church generally, and on throughout the Christian Era to the most recent directives of Rome on philosophy in priestly training.[7]

THE STUDY OF WISDOM

There is no question but that Socrates, Plato, and Aristotle had in mind a natural human science or discipline that penetrates beyond phenomena to abiding intelligible principles of reality as such. These intelligible principles comprise its proper object, distinct from the objects of the sciences and disciplines which are counted among the first six arts; and the rational insights into these principles and the understandings about the necessity of their existence if reality is to be explained and human life is to be understood are the fruit of its study and research. It was the conviction of these Greek thinkers that this rational discipline called philosophy opens up to man the study of wisdom and promises to provide the foundation for humanism specifically as such. It follows that this discipline which studies natural wisdom is indispensable to man in his quest for the happy life.[8]

---

[7] St. Augustine listed philosophy consistently throughout his life as the seventh of the seven liberal arts. See *Retractations* I, chap. 6, no. 3 (PL 32, 591). The documents of the Magisterium from Vatican I through Vatican II on the study of philosophy are numerous and consistent, down to the letter, dated January 29, 1972, from the Sacred Congregation for Catholic Education "To the Ordinaries of the World on the Study of Philosophy in Seminaries"; this letter is reprinted in *The Program of Priestly Formation* (Washington, DC: NCCB, 1976), 145–155. Cf. Battista Mondin, "Philosophy Necessary in Priestly Formation," *L'Osservatore Romano* English Edition (March 2, 1972), 11: "Those who are most exposed to the influence of Protestantism, or more exactly to a certain kind of Protestantism, for example that of Barth and Bonhoeffer, maintain that philosophy is useless or even harmful in priestly formation." As Mondin points out, summarizing the position of Vatican II and of the Holy See in this letter, the truth is exactly the opposite; theology has more need of philosophy today than ever before. But it must be the right kind of philosophy, taught in the right way: "It will not suffice to teach the history of philosophy" (ibid.). We shall return to this point below when the intervening discussion hopefully will have assisted in making this position more intelligible.

[8] Concern for human happiness, variously defined, was uppermost in the philosophical schools which developed as perhaps the most distinctive mark of the classical culture. See Ragnar Holte, *Beatitude et Sagesse: Saint Augustin et le problème de la fin de l'homme dans la philosphie ancienne* (Paris: Etudes Augustiniennes, 1962). Christian philosophy did not disavow this concern when it broke through to its more clear and lucid concept of God, and became able to see the truth with Augustine: *verus phi-*

How did the Greeks conceive the object which this discipline studies? "We are seeking the principles and causes of existing things," Aristotle answers, "by which I mean existing things *qua* existing."[9] "If there is anything eternal, immutable, and existing separately," he continues, "it must be studied by a speculative science. Not by physics . . . nor by mathematics, but by one that is prior to both. . . . If there are none but natural substances, physics will be the primary science. But if there is an immutable substance, the science which deals with it must be primary. Because it is primary, it is universal, and it is therefore concerned with the essence and properties of being *qua* being."[10] "If, then, as I shall try to show, there is a separate unchanging substance, the science of it is different from physics and mathematics. If there is such a substance, here surely is the divine, and the first and most authoritative principle. Evidently, then, there are three kinds of theoretical sciences: physics, mathematics, theology."[11]

In practice, Aristotle seems to have devoted his attention more to the substances visible in the cosmos than to rational theology. "We know a thing (e.g. man, fire) best when we know *what* it is," he goes on, "and not simply its quantity, quality, position, etcetera. . . . The ancient and everlasting question, 'What is being?' really amounts to 'What is substance?' It was substance that many of the earlier philosophers described as one or many, as numerically finite or infinite; so that it must be our first and principal, if not our *only* object."[12]

It is fundamentally important to recognize that philosophy did not spring forth from these Greek pioneers in its perfected form. Aristotle's definition, one can see, does not bear upon the *existence* of realities, as

---

losophus amator Die (*De civitate Dei* bk. 8, chap. 1). One can see this perhaps best in Augustine's *De beata vita,* the short gem among the Dialogues of Cassiciacum, those early works which earn for him the title of "Founder of Christian Philosophy." For Augustine, philosophy, always the culminating component of natural humane studies, is the "science of virtue and wisdom," as he terms it in his *De Magistro* 14.45 (PL 32, 1219).

9   John Warrington, trans., *Aristotle's Metaphysics* (London: Dent, 1956), 153.

10   Ibid., 154–155.

11   Ibid., 156. Warrington notes that Aristotle's reference is "probably . . . to a lost or never written" treatise on God for which the extant portions of the Metaphysics are preparatory. In any case Aristotle's intention of openness to the Supreme Being is clear.

12   Ibid., 167–168. Aristotle proceeds to study the various meanings of substance, always in the context of the visible cosmos: "Substance is most commonly recognized as belonging to bodies—animals and plants and their parts, and what is compounded of them, e.g., the physical universe and its parts (the stars, the moon, and the sun)" (169).

such, so much as on the *forms* in which realities are seen to exist as phenomena of this visible cosmos. His mind is a powerful one, to be sure, but he stands with his head turned downward to the things of this earth, to their substantial forms, or natures, or essences.

THE QUEST OF WISDOM

The quest of wisdom in classical philosophy does indeed attempt to relate these understandings regarding natures surrounding man to the nature of man himself, and thus to provide man with a way of life based upon wisdom. Philosophy offers a guide for personal living, and hence there is a practical outcome from philosophy for each man's personal history. But there is no sign of a reasoned analysis of the meaning and direction of human history in the large, nor any example of systematic application of philosophical principles to what is given in that other discipline among the same seven arts called history. The classical philosophy advances only speculations about the eternal recurrence of all earthly events in cycles like a Great Year, and not rational knowledge about the actual successions of the realities which constitute the visible cosmos. Furthermore, this natural discipline offers no specific information about the original beginnings of the universe, nor any knowledge of a final goal. When it speculates about a final conflagration, it seems to draw upon popular religious traditions, and in doing so includes the goal as merely the beginning of another cycle of the selfsame events. The Trojan War, Aristotle opines, will be fought over again, the same to the last detail.[13]

Such are the facts. Linked closely with this inability to reach a philosophy of history was the characteristic failure to recognize the Creator. The classical philosophy did not rise to the doctrine of Creation. Thus it ministered to the secularized condition which came to predominate in the classical culture. It fostered on the one hand a schism in the soul promoted by the separation between the disciplines of philosophy and

---

[13] On the Greek cyclical view of time, from which not even Aristotle was exempt, see Eric Voegelin, "The Modes of Time" in *Order and History*, vol. 4, *The Ecumenic Age* (Columbia, MO: University of Missouri Press, 2001); and Karl Lowith, *Meaning in History: The Theological Implications of the Philosophy of History* (Chicago: The University of Chicago Press, 1949); "To the Greek thinkers a philosophy of history would have been a contradiction in terms" (4). For Augustine's refutation of the cyclical view, see *De civitate Dei* bk. 12, chaps. 9–20; for his rejection of fate and defense of contingency under Providence, see ibid. bk. 5, chaps. 2–11.

history; and on the other hand there was its characteristic intellectual darkness due to its failure to recognize God the Creator.

Thus there was literally no contact between "philosophy" and "history," and the question whether "history," as such, falls within the formal object of that science which studies an abiding reality beyond the object of the empirical and mathematical sciences was not even raised. And when it did not ask whether philosophy has the power to perceive succession as such, in its intelligibility, so as to know the meaning and direction of the succession in time of the natural substances and human entities which constitute the cosmos, it failed to reach that branch of philosophy known today as the philosophy of history.

Under the influence of Christianity, philosophy was regenerated and renewed, so that Christian philosophers discoursed with a new power and lucidity on the things of God and the soul, rising to the philosophical concept of creation from nothingness. Did this evoke the philosophy of history in its modern sense? In any sense?[14]

---

[14] For the general contrast of Christian thinking with the pagan concept of time, see Oscar Cullmann, *Christ and Time: The Primitive Christian Conception of Time and History* (Philadelphia: The Westminster Press, 1950), esp. 51–60, "The Linear Conception of Time in the Revelatory History of the Bible as Contrasted with the Cyclical Conception of Hellenism." See note 7 in the epilogue for the discussion which followed Cullmann's study.

2

HEBREW AND CHRISTIAN
HISTORICAL UNDERSTANDING

C HRISTIAN culture is the historic reality which succeeds in the
West to the Graeco-Roman culture of classical antiquity.[1] It is
affiliated with that earlier civilization; qualitatively, however, it is quite

---

[1] See Christopher Dawson, *The Making of Europe: An Introduction to the History of
European Unity* (New York: Sheed and Ward, 1938). Two decades later when he had
come from England, full of hope for Catholic education in the United States, to a Pro-
fessorship at Harvard University in Boston, Dawson had to suffer an attack upon the
idea of Christian culture by a Catholic college professor, an episode which historians
of the future doubtless will footnote in their studies of the "Americanism" in religion
which was ripening as the twentieth century proceeded. The incident evoked Dawson's
book, *The Historic Reality of Christian Culture* (New York: Harper, 1960). Toynbee
agrees that Christian culture is both a reality and qualitatively different. Cf. Arnold
J. Toynbee, *A Study of History*, 2nd ed. (London: Oxford University Press, 1935),
1:57–58:

> When the moribund Empire fell, the ensuing "interregnum" gave the living
> Church an opportunity to perform an act of creation. The Church then
> played the part of a chrysalis out of which there emerged in the fullness of
> time a new society of the same species as the old society which had disap-
> peared—but disappeared without carrying away the Church in its ruin as it
> had carried away the Empire. The essence of the Christian Church, which at
> once differentiates it as an institution from the Roman Empire and explains
> how it was able to go on living and growing when the Empire perished, was
> the germ of creative power which it harbored. . . . The Church was intimately
> concerned and not just accidentally associated with the "affiliation" of our
> Western Society to the Hellenic Society. . . . It was the chrysalis out of which
> our Western Society emerged.

different from it. The essential reason for the difference is to be found among the Hebrews.

The Hebrew Fact stands as a historic reality in its own right. It is documented in the priestly annals of Jerusalem, the capital city of the Hebrews, known today as the historical books of the Old Testament and available everywhere today in the Bible. For these books are written "history," independent and indeed strikingly unique in their literary genre.[2] In form they go beyond the mere chronicles of the Mesopotamian and Egyptian cities; in content they center entirely upon God as operating in the events of the national history, putting this people descending from Abraham into a special relationship to Himself, called the Covenant or Testament, and thus making of it the chosen People of God with a new and unique purpose.[3]

THE DOCTRINE OF CREATION

These writings present God as the Thrice-Holy One, the Almighty, the Creator of heaven and earth. It would be difficult to overemphasize the universality of the doctrine of Creation in the pages of the Hebrew writings. Its history is a record of the interventions of God into the ongoing processes of human life, something that already belongs to Him because He made it and hence is in a position to rule and to guide its unfolding development. "Lord, Lord, King and Master of all things," a Hebrew prays in a national crisis, "everything is subject to your power. . . . Yes,

---

[2] There can be different literary kinds in the writing of history; the Gospels offer a variation in the Hebrew genre. Records of the past, other ways of describing the way things actually took place, *wie es eigentlich gewesen ist,* in Ranke's famous phrase, can be quite truthful without the "modern" literary genre with its weight of footnotes. And heavy scholarship can be quite aberrational in its understanding and interpretation of the facts which it documents. For a detailed discussion of this point with modern and contemporary bearing, see Voegelin, *The New Science of Politics,* 1–26. For a standard presentation of the Hebrew concept of history and historical writing, see Christopher R. North, *The Old Testament Interpretation of History* (London: The Epworth Press, 1954).

[3] See Vatican II, Dogmatic Constitution on Divine Revelation *Dei verbum* (November 18, 1965), §2, in Flannery, ed., *Vatican Council II,* 751: "This economy of Revelation is realized by deeds and words, which are intrinsically bound up with each other. As a result, the works performed by God in the history of salvation show forth and bear out the doctrine and realities signified by the words; the words, for their part, proclaim the works, and bring to light the mystery they contain."

you have made heaven and earth and all the marvels that are under heaven."[4] The Psalm which calls Israel to its daily prayer expresses the mind of the Hebrew people: "Come, let us praise Yahweh joyfully. . . . For Yahweh is a great God, a greater King than all other gods; from depths of earth to mountain top everything comes under his rule; the sea belongs to him, he made it, so does the land, he shaped this too. Come in, let us bow, prostrate ourselves, and kneel in front of Yahweh our maker, for this is our God, and we are the people he pastures, the flock that he guides."[5]

These instances, which could be multiplied indefinitely from the Bible, illustrate the profound difference between "history" as this people understood and wrote it, and the discipline cultivated under the same name by the Greeks and the Romans. This is history that records contact with the Supreme Being of the universe: at one and the same time, contact with the Creator of the cosmos and the Lord of history.

Rome in the conquest of her Empire was able to subjugate every city, snuffing out its local religious and political life, terminating its local priestly annals, replacing them with her own cult and code and educational system—save one city alone.[6] Jerusalem she could not conquer in this way of education and culture which she preferred. In the end she had to destroy Jerusalem utterly, pulling apart every stone of her buildings and running a plow over her site. And even then this remarkable nation refused to yield: it kept its treasure of these unique writings and continued its life clustered about its synagogues in every place, always hoping for the great return to Jerusalem and the rebuilding of that temple which Titus had destroyed. Each year, for centuries, the aspiration has been voiced: *"Next year in Jerusalem."*

---

[4] Esther 4:17. The standard treatises on the biblical theology of the Old Testament gather the relevant texts and synthesize this distinctive Hebrew doctrine of Creation. See, for example, P.F. Ceuppens, O.P., *De Deo Uno* (Rome: Marietti, 1949); Alfons Deissler, *Die Grundbotschaft des Alten Testaments*, 6th ed. (Freiburg: Herder, 1978); P. Van Imschoot, "God and the World," in *Theology of the Old Testament* (New York: Desclee, 1965), 1:86–108; and especially Gerhard von Rad, "The Place in the Theology of the Witness Concerning Creation," in *Old Testament Theology* (New York: Harper and Row, 1962), 1:136–153,

[5] Psalms 95 (Jerusalem Bible; Psalms 94 in the older numeration); this psalm is the *Invitatorium* to prayer used daily in the *Liturgia Horarum* of the Catholic Church.

[6] See Fustel de Coulanges, "Rome Everywhere Destroys the Municipal System" and "The Conquered Nations successively enter the Roman City," in *The Ancient City* (New York: Doubleday Anchor Books, 1956), 374–388.

HISTORICAL SUCCESSION

What was (and is) unique about this durable Hebrew Fact? It was the paradoxical understanding of itself as provisional and temporary. Moses, and after him all the prophets, wrote of a Coming One who would establish a new and final Testament. "The scepter shall not depart from Judah . . . until he come to whom it belongs, and to him shall be the obedience of the peoples" (Gen 49:10). "I will shake all nations, so that the treasures of all nations shall come in, and I will fill this house with splendor, says the LORD of hosts" (Hag 2:7). "Behold, I send my messenger to prepare the way before me, and the Lord whom you seek will suddenly come to his temple; the messenger of the covenant in whom you delight, behold, he is coming, says the LORD of hosts. But who can endure the day of his coming . . . ? . . . I will draw near to you for the judgment. . . ." (Mal 3:1–5). Thus the Hebrews envisaged a vast religious succession in human history, descending parallel to the succession of the politico-cultural Empires of the Gentiles, but qualitatively quite different from them: "O LORD, . . . to you shall the nations come from the ends of the earth" (Jer 16:19).

"My heart overflows with a goodly theme," Psalm 45 sings, describing an everlasting throne and addressing a queen in gold from Ophir: "Hear, O daughter, consider, and incline your ear; forget your people and your father's house . . . The people of Tyre will court your favor with gifts, the richest of the people with all kinds of wealth. . . . Instead of your fathers shall be your sons; you will make them princes in all the earth" (Psalm 45:1, 10–12, 16). The Hebrews looked forward to some kind of universal sway, *toto orbe terrarum,* in terms which match those of Polybius above on Rome's empire over "almost the whole world."

A COMING ONE

No theme is more common or more characteristic of the Hebrew writings than this prophetic expectation of a new historical order in which a new covenant or testament with all nations will replace the present one with the Hebrew nation. And all the peoples, including the Hebrews, will be renewed in this coming dispensation. Let one passage from the prophets serve as an example:

> And I will vindicate the holiness of my great name, which has
> been profaned among the nations, and which you have pro-
> faned among them; and the nations will know that I am the
> LORD, says the Lord GOD, when through you I vindicate my
> holiness before their eyes. For I will take you from the nations,
> and gather you from all the countries, and bring you into your
> own land. I will sprinkle clean water upon you, and you shall
> be clean from all your uncleannesses, and from all your idols I
> will cleanse you. A new heart I will give you, and a new spirit I
> will put within you; and I will take out of your flesh the heart
> of stone and give you a heart of flesh. And I will put my spirit
> within you, and cause you to walk in my statutes and be careful
> to observe my ordinances. You shall dwell in the land which I
> gave to your fathers; and you shall be my people, and I will be
> your God. (Ezek 36:23–28)

Always this new and universal religious dispensation is expected to be
the work of the Coming One.

It is important to recognize the universality of this understanding of
succession, meaning, and direction in human affairs. The Hebrews professed as basic articles of their faith the origin of all mankind by creation
of the first human pair, and the fall of all mankind in a sin of that first man.
Their writings and their national religion transcend their own national
origin in Abraham. The Coming One was to be like Moses, indeed, but
not a new Moses or even a new Abraham. He was to be the New Adam,
from whom a new race and kind of man would proceed and populate the
earth, new men with hearts of flesh instead of hearts of stone.

JESUS CHRIST

Jesus Christ is the world-historical figure who intervenes at this point
with transforming power over human thought upon the meaning and
direction of universal history. He appeared as a rabbi, or teacher, according to the accepted pattern among the Hebrews. The key to the situation
emerges in the very beginning of His *talmudim,* when His group of disciples clustered about Him, attaching themselves to Him as students in
the common didactic procedure of the day.

John the Baptist pointed Him out to his own disciples, and two of
them went to explore. "Jesus turned, and saw them following, and said

to them 'What do you seek?' and they said to him, 'Rabbi' (which means Teacher) 'where are you staying?' He said to them 'Come and see.'" They stayed with Him the rest of that day, and forthwith began to contact and enlist their companions: "We have found him of whom Moses in the law and also the prophets wrote, Jesus of Nazareth, the son of Joseph" (Jn 1:37–46).[7]

The Teacher proceeded with an intensive program of teaching and formation designed to prepare His twelve ordinary Hebrew men, outdoor men of the common people, men with only the common elementary schooling of the Synagogue, to receive His own mission and to be sent out with it to all nations. "Go therefore and make disciples of all nations, baptizing them in the name of the Father and of the Son and of the Holy Spirit, teaching them to observe all that I have commanded you; and behold, I am with you always, to the close of the age." (Mt 28:19–20).[8]

---

[7] Thus the disciples from the very beginning recognized Jesus as the Coming One, and this was their experience of His presence and activity throughout their time with Him as His students. That the final events of mankind began to occur with the first preaching, or better, *heralding* of the news that the Kingdom of God is now at hand, is recognized accurately by L. G. Patterson, *God and History in Early Christian Thought* (London: Black, 1967), 9: "Such a classic description of the first preaching [as that in Mark 1:14–15 and Matthew 4:17] . . . arises from a powerful apprehension, attributable to no one but Jesus Himself, of the immediate manifestation of divine power in the happenings of the present." This insight underlies the breaking of demonic power in the Gospels and the frequent references to the Hebrew prophets, especially Isaiah and Daniel. "It is inherent in the appeal made to Isaiah 29:18ff, in support of taking not only the healings but the preaching of the Gospel to the poor as proof that the 'Coming One,' the agency in the establishment of the Kingdom, is even now present to perform His redemptive functions (Mt 11:4–6; Lk. 4:18–19)" (ibid.). Thus the Christian Era, however protracted, is the period of the ending of this world.

[8] The Gospels and the Acts of the Apostles always have been considered historical books of the Bible, continuing the literary genre of historiography among the Hebrews. See John L. McKenzie, "History; Historical Writing," *Dictionary of the Bible* (Milwaukee: Bruce, 1965), 360–363; and "Gospel," ibid., 320–323, quoting the happy phrase of Leon-Dufour which calls the Gospels "catechetical booklets reporting history." The defense of the historicity of the historical books of the Bible always has been an essential aspect of intellectual life among Christians. Gnosticism, both in antiquity and in its resurrected form which has become common in the twentieth century, characteristically seeks to evade and to deny the historical element in Christianity. The Early Church defended this historicity tooth and nail, for instance Irenaeus' *Against the Heresies*. There is a consistent series of documents of the Magisterium from Leo XIII to the present on this point. Cf., in particular, the constitution *Dei verbum* of Vatican II. For an example of the manner in which younger, post-Conciliar scholars are coming to grips with the contemporary philosophical Gnosticism, particularly in Bultmann's

His teaching came to a sudden shattering end in the ignominious crucifixion. It resulted directly from betrayal. He died and was buried. Then on the third day the illuminating and transforming fact of His Resurrection from the dead burst upon His scattered and demoralized followers. The effect was of course electrifying, for His disciples were convinced from His appearances that it was really He, alive again after death. But not all accepted their witness easily. "Unless I see in his hands the print of the nails," Thomas maintained stoutly, "'. . . I will not believe. Eight days later, . . . The doors were shut, but Jesus came and stood among them . . . Then he said to Thomas, 'Put your finger here, and see my hands . . . do not be faithless, but believing.' Thomas answered him, 'My Lord and my God!'" (Jn 20:25–28).

THE PROFESSION OF THE APOSTOLIC FAITH

This is one of the original forms of the Profession of the Apostolic Faith. Many instances of this nucleus of the Profession are scattered through the pages of the New Testament, the sudden and dramatic conclusion of the Old Testament, as men everywhere find it to this day in the Bible. Sent by the Risen Lord to teach all nations and to baptize them in the names of the Three Persons in the unity of Yahweh's Godhead, the Apostles now recognized with new clarity that Jesus Himself had taught and trained and formed them precisely for this mission when they were with Him in His rabbinical school.

It is readily understandable, as a simple practical necessity in taking up their assignment, that they needed a brief summary of the news about Jesus, His events and His doctrine on the Three Persons in the One God of the Hebrews. This summary gathered the content of their evangelization into a set of articles which state the apostolic Faith. This was the pattern or standard of their catechetical teaching which prepared men and women for Baptism.[9] The profession of this same Faith at Baptism

---

version of it, cf. John F. McCarthy, *The Science of Historical Theology* (Rome: Prop. Mariana, 1976).

[9] See Romans 6:17, where St. Paul's original Greek refers to the *typon didaches* which had been delivered to the converts by the apostolic program of evangelization and catechesis, and which they obeyed from the heart. Jerome translates in the Vulgate: "in eam formam doctrinae in quam traditi estis"; the New American Bible: "that rule of teaching which was imparted to you"; and the Jerusalem Bible: "you submitted without

was required from the beginning for the reception of members into what He had called "My Church," and it has been required consistently across the centuries to the present.

This official summary of the Apostolic Faith is known popularly today, in a particular verbal form at home among peoples whose languages derive from the Latin, as the Apostles' Creed. It is a marvelously compact statement of the Christian message about Jesus, relating Him, His Person and His work, to the Three Divine Persons, and stating that everything about Him took place "according to the Scriptures," meaning the fulfillment of the Hebrew Scriptures which Christians call the Old Testament. For everything about Jesus, Peter insists, took place "according to the definite plan and foreknowledge of God" (Acts 2:23). The Profession of the Apostolic Faith, furthermore, recognizes two comings of Jesus Christ: this first one, now accomplished and completed, and a second one in glory, at the end of this present world and its history, as the Judge of the living and the dead.[10]

---

reservation to the creed you were taught." This creedal standard or pattern which gave the catechetical teaching program of the Apostles its form and its content was not yet fixed into one set of words known at that time as "The Apostles' Creed." That particular set of words emerged later from the life and practice of the Church. But the substance was proclaimed in evangelization, taught in catechesis, and professed at Baptism, constantly and consistently forward from the Apostolic origins of the Church. In fact, this vital practice is the dynamic process of the ongoing apostolicity of the Church, the life-process which constitutes the Catholic Fact and builds it into visibility in human history. See J.N.D. Kelly, *Early Christian Creeds*, 3rd ed. (London: Longman, 1972).

[10] The Apostles' Profession of Faith or "Creed" was a summary made officially by the teaching authority of the Church of the essential facts reported in the historical books of the Bible, and hence it itself bore directly upon history. In one of the earliest extant allusions to this Profession, written when the Apostle John was still alive, St. Ignatius of Antioch stresses this historicity by using the words "really," "in reality" and "truly":

> Stop your ears, therefore, when anyone speaks to you at variance with Jesus Christ, the Son of God, who was descended from David, and was also of Mary; who was truly begotten of God and of the Virgin, but not after the same manner. For indeed God and man are not the same. He truly assumed a body; for "the Word was made flesh" and lived on earth without sin. . . . He did in reality both eat and drink. He was crucified and died under Pontius Pilate. He really, and not merely in appearance, was crucified, and died, in the sight of beings in heaven, and on earth, and under the earth. . . . He descended, indeed, into Hades alone, but He arose accompanied by a multitude. . . . He also rose again in three days, the Father raising Him up; and after spending forty days with the apostles, He was received up to the Father. . . . Mary then did truly conceive a body which had God inhabiting it. And God the Word was truly born of the Virgin, having clothed Himself with a body of like passions with our own . . . and was really born, as we also are. . . . And when He

THE NEW CENTER OF HISTORY

It is clear that this Profession of the Apostolic Faith contains a new and specifically Christian understanding of the universal history of mankind. In fact, the event to which it bears witness and makes known by its witness, the Incarnation of the Supreme Being and the redemption of mankind on His Cross, changes the character of history itself.

"From the moment that it takes place," writes Gigon, "it necessarily takes its position as the center of all history, as the midpoint in the strict sense, insofar as it simultaneously establishes the beginning and ending points of universal history to which it itself as midpoint is related."[11] The historical time which reaches from the beginning, the creation of the world and its history, to the midpoint, stands revealed as a time of preparation precisely for this central event. This is the meaning of the phrase "according to the Scriptures" in the Profession of Faith. "And this preparatory movement of history forward toward the Incarnation of God correlates with the subsequent movement of history from this event toward the End of the World."[12]

---

had lived among men for thirty years, He was baptized by John, really, and not in appearance; and when He had preached the Gospel three years, and done signs and wonders, He who was Himself the Judge was judged by the Jews, falsely so called, and by Pilate the governor; was scourged, was smitten on the cheek, was spit upon; He wore a crown of thorns and a purple robe; He was condemned: He was crucified in reality, and not in appearance, not in imagination, not in deceit. He really died, and was buried, and rose from the dead. . . . The Father, therefore, who raised Him up, will also raise us up through Him, apart from whom no one will attain to true life. For He says, "I am the life; he that believeth in me, even though he die, shall live: and every one that liveth and believeth in me, even though he die, shall live forever." (Ignatius of Antioch, *Epistle to the Trallians*, chaps. 9–10, in Alexander Roberts and James Donaldson, eds., *The Ante-Nicene Fathers* [New York: Scribner's, 1926], 1:69–71)

[11] Olof Gigon, *Die antike Kultur und das Christentum* (Gütersloh, DE: Verlagshaus Gerd Mohn, 1969), 145. This is the intellectual justification for Christocentrism in Catechetics; cf. the *General Catechetical Directory,* nos. 40 and 88, on the "religious way of thinking" which is prerequisite for catechesis with adolescents and adults. This Christocentrism literally has no real meaning apart from the understanding of history under analysis here; for either Jesus Christ is really, truly, in reality (to use the words and witness of Ignatius of Antioch) the midpoint of universal history, or Christianity must be reinterpreted according to the project of the Modernists. Cf. the comprehensive work of Cullmann, *Christ and Time.*

[12] Ibid., 146. The Bible has numerous references to the End, including entire chapters in the Gospels which summarize what Jesus taught about it; and one of its books, *Revela-*

It is fundamentally important to note that the Profession of the Apostolic Faith, by its first article, continues and fulfills the Hebrew doctrine of creation. It is through this same Eternal Son, now incarnate, that God the Father created heaven and earth, meaning all things visible and invisible. The plan which the Almighty put into His creation is a plan for the redemption of mankind.[13] This is accomplished through the sending of His Eternal Son, and then through the consequent sending of the Holy Spirit from both the Father and the Son upon the new entity which Jesus organized as a part of his teaching program and called "my church" (Mt 16:18). Hence the threefold division of the Apostles' Profession and its resulting masterful synthesis of the meaning and direction of history as salvation history, built by God into reality as an integral part of creation as such.[14] And it is the third article, on

---

tion or the *Apocalypse,* is devoted *ex professo* to it. From this foundation in the Scriptures the theological treatise on *The Last Things* has been developed across the centuries. Cf. Augustine, *De civitate Dei* bks. 19–22; Thomas Aquinas, *Summa Theologica* III, qq. 69–99; L. Billot, *Quaestiones de Novissimis* (Rome: The Gregorian University Press, 1924); Antonius Piolanti, *De Novissimis* (Rome: Marietti, 1946, 1950); Franz Mussner, *Was lehrt Jesus über das Ende der Welt?* (Freiburg: Herder, 1958). (Now in English: *What did Jesus Teach about the End of the World?* [Ann Arbor: Word of Life, 1974]).

[13] See John 1:1–14: "In the beginning was the Word. . . . All things were made through him and without him was made nothing that has been made. . . . And the Word was made flesh and dwelt among us." For the bearing of this upon catechetical teaching in the Church, see the *General Catechetical Directory,* no. 51: "The truth of creation is not to be presented simply as a truth standing by itself, torn from the rest, but as something which is in fact ordered to the salvation wrought by Jesus Christ." This is another way of stating the principle regarding the philosophy of history which is developed in the present study: this branch of philosophy is unique in that it correlates with the doctrine of creation, knowing (philosophically) that the Creator would have some kind of plan, and open therefore (i.e., coordinated with theology) to some word from on high about the matter.

[14] The Epistles of St. Paul mark the beginning of Christian thought about history and the divine plan in history. The centering of the plan upon the historical Jesus as the Eternal Son, Lord of men and their history, is the theme of them all, and both the beginning and the end of universal history recur throughout the Pauline writings. The plan itself is summarized in magnificent sweeping passages, for example Acts 17:22–34; Ephesians 1; Colossians 1:1–2, 7; Romans 9, 10, 11. Vatican II, twenty centuries later, teaches the same understanding of universal history: cf. Pastoral Constitution on the Church in the Modern World *Gaudium et spes* (December 7, 1965), §45: "The Word of God, through whom all things were made, was made flesh, so that as a perfect man he could save all men and sum up all things in himself. The Lord is the goal of human history, the focal point of the desires of history and civilization, the center of mankind. . . . Animated and drawn together in his Spirit we press onwards on our journey towards the consummation of history . . ." (in Flannery, *Vatican Council II,*

the work of the Holy Spirit raising up a standard for the nations (cf. Is 11:12), which bears directly upon the Christian understanding of universal history. The Apostles, particularly Sts. Peter and Paul, made this standard, the Catholic Church, visible on the stage of history already in the first century by their energetic apostolate. Quickly they moved out from the original base at Jerusalem to Antioch and then to Rome. Soon afterward the fourth original Apostolic See was established at Alexandria, an action traditionally attributed to St. Mark, who had been with St. Peter at Rome as his younger associate. For the Apostles did not share an erroneous opinion on the imminence of the Second Coming which was widespread among Christians in the decades immediately following the crucifixion and the Resurrection. The Apostles themselves were careful to clarify the official teaching of the Church to the contrary. As St. Paul explains to the Thessalonians, the day of the Lord is not yet near at hand:

> Let no one deceive you in any way; for that day will not come, unless the rebellion comes first, and the man of lawlessness is revealed, the son of perdition, who opposes and exalts himself against every so-called god or object of worship, so that he takes his seat in the temple of God, proclaiming himself to be God. Do you not remember that when I was still with you I told you this? And you know what is restraining him now so that he may be revealed in his time. (2 Thess 2:3–6)

Thus the Apostles saw the time before them as divided into two moments: first, the period of the mission to all peoples and nations with the Christian message; and after that, the mysterious events leading directly and immediately to the Second Coming. For the Apostles, the obvious answer regarding the delay was to use the time for the formation of the Christian assemblies or *ecclesiae,* the churches being actively organized ever more widely out into every place from the four original Apostolic Sees. St. Paul, the Apostle to the Gentiles, was witnessing already the conversion of the pagan peoples to God in the universal Church of Jesus Christ: for him it was already a present fact which he was able to see and to experience. And he states clearly his understanding of it.

---

947). This teaching emphasizes the need for research on the relationship between philosophy and theology according to *Optatam totius,* §14, a relationship mediated by a correct understanding of the nature and role of philosophy of history.

THE CATHOLIC FACT

A New Israel is being formed by means of these *ecclesiae,* an eschato-
logical Israel arising out of Abraham's seed and formed out of Jews and
Gentiles without the distinctions and national customs of the Old Testament.[15] The Hebrew Torah is recognized as preparatory for this new
fact. St. Paul, and the entire Early Church with him, recognizes what
is beginning to take place as the fulfillment of the Hebrew Scriptures
in their prophecy of the calling of the Gentiles into the world-wide
New Testament which is to succeed in the time of the Coming One.
The emergence of this New Israel on the stage of universal history, furthermore, is in turn preparatory to coming events regarding the Hebrew
nation itself. For the refusal of this people to join the universal movement of the Gentile nations into the unity of the New Israel is seen by
the Apostles as an apostasy which is itself a fulfillment of prophecy; and
St. Paul in his profound chapters to the Romans looks forward to the
conversion of a remnant of the Hebrew people sometime in the future,
on the eve of the final manifestation of divine power.[16]

This is the substance of the Christian understanding of history. The
Fathers of the Church from Justin through Augustine to Gregory the
Great will develop it greatly, but they will not change it.

The Catholic Fact emerges in this way and becomes visible on the
panorama of universal history. It results from the apostolate, through
the distinct yet interrelated processes of evangelization and catechesis. It
is the work of the catechumenate, the apostolic teaching program which
explained the creedal facts about Jesus *secundum Scripturas,* as the fulfillment of the Hebrew Scriptures, and then baptized into membership
in the New Israel of God and its way of life. Thus the Catholic Fact
follows upon the Hebrew Fact, and is one thing with it in the continuity of religious succession, the succession of the Testaments as an actual
happening of history.

---

[15] See Romans 3:31–4, 25; Galatians 3:1–19.
[16] See Patterson, *God and History,* 12. See Romans 9, 10, and 11 on the problem of
the rejection of Israel during the times of the Gentiles and the future conversion of a
remnant of the Jewish people toward the end of history; cf. Erik Peterson, *Die Kirche
aus Juden und Heiden* (Salzburg: Verlag Anton Pustet, 1933).

3

THE PATRISTIC
UNDERSTANDING OF HISTORY

THOUGHT about the fact and the meaning of this succession in time was an essential component of Catholic intellectual life from the beginning.[1] In fact, the early Christian thinkers were keenly aware of their own participation in the fulfillment of the Hebrew prophecies; they actually saw the conversion of the Graeco-Roman world to God in the universal Church of Jesus Christ and experienced it personally.

ST. JUSTIN MARTYR

"We will now offer proof," writes St. Justin Martyr in the second century, regarding Jesus Christ,

> ... not trusting mere assertions, but being of necessity persuaded by those who prophesied [of Him] before these things came to pass, for with our own eyes we behold things that have happened and are happening just as they were predicted. ... There were, then, among the Jews certain men who were prophets of

---

[1] For a comprehensive presentation of the evidence for this statement, see Patterson, *God and History*; also Charles Norris Cochrane, *Christianity and Classical Culture: A Study of Thought and Action from Augustus to Augustine* (New York: Oxford University Press, 1944); and Gigon, *Die antike Kultur*. Whether or in what sense this Christian thinking is "philosophy of history" is a question still to be considered in the present study.

God, through whom the prophetic Spirit published beforehand things that were to come to pass, before ever they happened. . . . In these books, then, of the prophets we found Jesus our Christ foretold as coming, born of a virgin, growing up to a man's estate, and healing every disease and every sickness, and raising the dead, and being hated, and unrecognized, and crucified, and dying, and rising again, and ascending into heaven, and being called, the Son of God. We find it also predicted that certain persons should be sent by Him into every nation to publish these things, and that rather among the Gentiles [than among the Jews] men should believe in Him.[2]

This is the experience of the Catholic Fact as it is in the process of being built into history. In further chapters of his *First Apology,* Justin elaborates in detail upon the Hebrew prophecies, explaining that Moses predicted Christ (Gen 49:10), that Isaiah foretold the manner and place of His birth, that the prophets in general foresaw details of His life, His crucifixion, and His life in heaven after death, and that His rejection by the Jews and the destruction of Jerusalem had been foretold. "When the Spirit of prophecy speaks as predicting things that are to come to pass," Justin continues,

He speaks in this way: "For out of Zion shall go forth the law, and the word of the Lord from Jerusalem. And He shall judge among the nations . . ." (Is 2:3). And that it did so come to pass, we can convince you. For from Jerusalem there went out into the world, men, twelve in number, and these illiterate, of no ability in speaking: but by the power of God they proclaimed to every race of men that they were sent by Christ to teach to all the word of God; and we who formerly used to murder one another do not only now refrain from making war on our enemies, but also, that we may not lie or deceive our examiners, willingly die confessing Christ.[3]

The fulfillment is really happening: the Gospel is being heralded out of Jerusalem. It is an event of contemporary history for Justin, who simply

---

[2] Justin Martyr, *The First Apology of Justin,* in M. Dods trans., *The Writings of Justin Martyr and Athenagoras* (Edinburgh: Clark, 1867), 32–33.
[3] Ibid., 40.

reports the manner of seeing and judging the course of events which was general among the early Christians.

Then he gives the characteristic Christian linear orientation toward the anticipated end of history.

> Since, then, we prove that all things which have already happened had been predicted by the prophets before they came to pass, we must necessarily believe also that those things which are in like manner predicted, but are yet to come to pass, shall certainly happen. . . . For the prophets have proclaimed two advents of His: the one, that which is already past, when He came as a dishonored and suffering man; but the second, when, according to prophecy, He shall come from heaven with glory, accompanied by His angelic host, when also he shall raise the bodies of all men who have lived. . . .[4]

Justin proceeds to cite Ezekiel 37; Isaiah 45, 46, 63, 64; and Zechariah 12. "Though we could bring forward many other prophecies," he concludes, "we forbear, judging these sufficient for the persuasion of those who have ears to hear and understand. . . . So many things therefore, as these, when they are seen with the eye, are enough to produce conviction and belief . . ."[5]

TERTULLIAN

Justin was a seminal thinker whose fundamental insights on the meaning and direction of universal history were developed by Irenaeus and the Greek Fathers, and by Tertullian, from whom they passed to the great Latins, especially Augustine.

---

[4] Ibid., 50–51.

[5] Ibid., 52–53. Justin Martyr is remarkable for his balanced and comprehensive contact with Graeco-Roman culture in both of the disciplines, *historia* and *philosophia,* on the program of the *paideia.* The Greek Fathers were more one-sided, making contact chiefly with *philosophia.* Patterson in the work already cited is noteworthy for his positive evaluation of the Latin Fathers, for their characteristically sharper insight into *historia,* and especially for their ability to correlate it with *philosophia.* Augustine's *De civitate Dei* is the abiding masterpiece which illustrates this point—a point which indicates the original fountainhead of the branch of philosophy known since Voltaire as the philosophy of history.

"That which will teach us [regarding the divinity of the Sacred Scriptures] is right at hand," writes Tertullian; "namely, the world, all time, all events. All that is now happening was foretold . . ."[6] And he cites the troubles which were besetting the Roman Empire in his day, the same domestic social evils and foreign barbian inroads which the pagans were attributing to the Christian refusal to worship the gods of Rome. "Even while we experience these happenings," he continues, "they are being read; while we recall them, they are being fulfilled. The actual fulfillment of the prophecy is, I dare say, sufficient indication of its inspired nature."[7]

Tertullian proceeds to the Hebrew doctrine on the Coming One, and the fulfillment of it in the birth, life, death, and Resurrection of Jesus of Nazareth. Then he takes up the second aspect of Hebrew prophecy, the apostolate to the nations which is to raise up a new Israel. "The disciples, too, hearkening to the command of God, their Master, spread throughout the world, and, after enduring with constancy much suffering from the persecution of the Jews, finally, because of the savage cruelty of Nero, sowed the seed of Christian blood at Rome . . ."[8]

Tertullian then takes up the burning question of his day, whether Rome's prosperity and greatness are being jeopardized by the Christian movement away from the worship of her pagan gods, toward the worship of Yahweh, the God of the Hebrews incarnate in Jesus of Nazareth. The pagan deities did not give Rome her empire, Tertullian answers; it is a work of the Christian God who is the Lord of history, who has a providential control over the rise, the fall and the succession of earthly empires. "Watch out, then," Tertullian warns the pagan Romans, "lest the one who dispenses kingdoms . . . and who has made the world a unified system of times has ordained changes in the ruling powers during certain periods in the course of time; lest He under whom the race of men once lived before there were cities at all be the One who raises cities and destroys them."[9] "In our case," he continues, "we pray for

---

[6]   Tertullian, *Apology*, in Rudolph Arbesmann, Emily Joseph Daly, and Edwin A. Quain, trans., *Tertullian: Apologetical Works* (New York: Fathers of the Church, 1950), 60.

[7]   Ibid. Tertullian uses Justin's argument for the Christian vision of the end of history: "In consequence of all this, it is safe for us to trust in the future, also, which we may consider already proved, since it has been predicted as well as events which each day are being proved true. The same voices give it utterance; the same literature records it; the same spirit animates it. All time is *one* to prophecy which foretells the future."

[8]   Ibid., 66.

[9]   Ibid., 81.

the welfare of the emperors to the eternal God, the true God, the living God . . ."[10] "There is also another, even greater, obligation for us to pray for the emperors; yes, even for the continuance of the empire in general and for Roman interests. We realize that the tremendous force which is hanging over the whole world, and the very end of the world with its threat of dreadful afflictions, is arrested for a time by the continued existence of the Roman Empire. This event we have no desire to experience, and, in praying that it may be deferred, we favor the continuance of Rome."[11]

ST. AUGUSTINE

St. Augustine, who in so many ways synthesizes the thought of the Early Church in his person and his work, describes most copiously and vividly this eyewitnessing and experience of the Catholic Fact. For him, it is nothing else than the *metanoia,* the conversion of the Roman Empire, the Graeco-Roman education and culture (and for him, this was effectively the whole of mankind) to God in the Catholic Church. He builds upon this Catholic Fact as something given in history, that understand-

---

[10] Ibid., 85.

[11] Ibid., 88. The "obstacle" or "hindrance" in 2 Thessalonians 2:7, which is holding off the end of the world and providing time for the Worldmission, was taken by Tertullian, and by the Fathers perhaps generally, to refer to the Roman Empire, which under providence was to last until the end is at hand. Cf. Tertullian, *Ad Scapulam* II: "As long as the world shall last . . . so long the Roman Empire will last." From the Patristic Age this view of things passed into the common thought of the Christian people, witnessed for example by the Roman proverb: "As long as the Colosseum stands, Rome shall stand; when the Colosseum falls, Rome will fall; when Rome falls, the world will fall" (Cf. PL 95, 543). Cf. Patterson, *God and History*, 61: "Tertullian . . . accepts the view that Rome is the last of the world empires—a view which Christians had always shared with Rome itself, albeit on somewhat different grounds . . ." John Henry Newman held the same view throughout the Nineteenth Century: cf. *Discussions and Arguments on Various Subjects* (London: Longman, Green, 1899), 50: "It is not clear that the Roman Empire is gone. Far from it: the Roman Empire in the view of prophecy, remains even to this day . . . 'that which withholdeth' still exists." Also ibid., p. 81: "It is difficult to say whether the Roman Empire is gone or not; in one sense it is gone, for it is divided into kingdoms; in another sense, it is not, for the date cannot be assigned at which it came to an end, and much might be said in various ways to show that it may be considered still existing, though in a mutilated and decayed state." Thus Newman. What he says is significant for the analysis conducted by an authentic and open philosophy of history, and will be pertinent to considerations below in the value judgment upon modernity as apostasy from God.

ing of history which has its abiding masterpiece in the City of God.

It is of course not possible here to do an extended study of Augustine from this point of view. Only the salient features of his thinking can be outlined, together with some indications for further research. Perhaps the best introduction to his personal view and experience of the Catholic Fact is his treatise on *The True Religion,* conceived among the Dialogues of Cassiciacum and written about three years after his own conversion, while still a layman, for his friend and patron Romanianus.

Augustine sketches what a great *metanoia* it would be if the peoples were to "change their minds and seek the one God who alone is superior to our minds, and by whom clearly every soul and the whole world has been created."[12] Plato aspired to something like this, Augustine continues, but inefficaciously. "Some great and divine man" would have to intervene, "to persuade the peoples that such things were to be at least believed if they could not grasp them with the mind."[13]

"Now this very thing has come to pass," Augustine concludes. "It is celebrated in books and documents. From one particular region of the earth in which alone the one God was worshiped and where alone such a man could be born, chosen men were sent throughout the entire world . . . Their sound teaching has been confirmed and they have left to posterity a world illumined."[14]

It would be difficult to state more succinctly the perception of the Catholic Fact as a reality observed and experienced. It is the Catholic Church seen as a dynamic turning movement of the peoples that had been gathered into the Roman Empire. It is their "conversion to the one true God . . . These things [the Gospel teachings] are read to the peoples throughout all the earth . . . as far afield as among barbarian nations. . . . All over the inhabited world . . . Multitudes enter upon this way of life from every race . . ."[15]

Augustine is careful to distinguish between what we today call "philosophy" and "theology." In his short treatise *On Faith in Things Unseen,* he introduces the Church as calling attention to her own presence and reality, fulfilling the Hebrew expectation of a New Testament embracing the Gentile peoples. This is something the unbeliever can see and

---

[12] Augustine, *De vera religione,* in J. H. S. Burleigh, trans., *St. Augustine: Of True Religion* (Chicago: Regnery, 1959), 2.

[13] Ibid., 4.

[14] Ibid., 5.

[15] Ibid., 7–8.

know. "Truly, this you have not seen [namely, the events of the historical Jesus in Palestine], but you do see His Church."[16]

> Those who were believers at that time in the land of Juda learned of the marvelous birth of Christ of a Virgin, learned of His Passion, Resurrection, and Ascension, and being present there learned all His divine words and the deeds firsthand. These things you have not seen: therefore, you refuse to believe them. . . . therefore; direct your attention to them; reflect upon the things which you behold, which are not narrated to you as of the past, nor foretold to you as of the future, but are clearly demonstrated to you as present. Now, . . . do you think it is either a little or no divine miracle that all mankind runs its course in the name of One Crucified? . . . You are seeing what was prophesied in Ps. 21 [that] *all the ends of the earth shall be converted to the Lord . . . and he shall have dominion over the nations.*[17]

THE CONVERSION OF THE ROMAN EMPIRE

The Catholic Fact, the historical reality of the Church as a sudden illumination visible in the whole world, *in toto orbe terrarum,* is the constant intellectual background for all the writings of Augustine. It recurs in his sermons, particularly in the *Enarrationes in psalmos.* It is the fundamental theme of the *De civitate Dei,* the treatise which seals the intellectual victory of Christian thinking within the Catholic Faith

---

[16] Augustine, *On Faith in Things Unseen,* Deferrari-McDonald, trans. (New York: Fathers of the Church, 1947), 2:461. *Me attendite, vobis dicit Ecclesia.* And Augustine correlates the present reality of the Church, which an unbeliever can see by his natural reason, with Psalms 45: *Ego sum Ecclesia de qua in eodem psalmo dicitur. . . . Constitues eos principes super omnem terram.* Ibid., 3:5. The key concept here in the Psalmist's prophecy is that of the *whole* earth, *all* the peoples, the *entire* Gentile world. For Augustine, like all educated men of his day, the Roman Empire was this entire world. This is what recurs constantly in Augustine's description of his own experience and thought regarding the actual fulfillment *toto orbe terrarum* of the Hebrew expectation.

[17] Ibid., 462–463. St. Thomas Aquinas stresses this same divine miracle, the conversion of the pagan world of classical antiquity to God in the Catholic Church, in his catechetical explanation of the Apostles' Creed.

over the ancient pagan philosophy, education, and culture.[18] In Book III
of his *De doctrina christiana* Augustine explains in detail his evaluation
of this worldwide conversion taking place before the eyes of classical
antiquity.[19] Citing Ezekiel 36:23–28, he concludes to the Catholic Fact
which he is experiencing: "Now that this is a prophecy of the New Testament, to which pertain not only a remnant of that one nation . . . but
also the other nations which were promised to their fathers and our
fathers; and that there is here a promise of that washing of regeneration
which, as we see, is now imparted to all nations, no one who looks into
the matter can doubt."[20]

It remains to sketch briefly Augustine's understanding of the
meaning and direction of universal history, the result of his reflection
upon these two Facts, the Hebrew and the Catholic.

In the first place, completing the work of Julius Africanus and Eusebius, Augustine brought *historia* and *philosophia,* distinct disciplines
on the curriculum of the classical Liberal Arts, into a correlation which
the fragmented pagan mind was unable to achieve. This becomes clear
in his very concept of history with its openness to the Lord of history
by means of the new philosophical recognition of the doctrine of creation. "When the past arrangements of men are recounted in historical
narration," he writes, "we must not consider history itself among those
human institutions. For, things which have now passed away and cannot

---

[18] For the *Enarrationes,* see M. Pontet, *L'Éxégèse de Saint Augustin Prédicateur* (Paris:
Aubier, 1945). Cf., for example, *En. in ps. 47: Omnia antea prophetata sunt.* (CCL
38, 543). For *De civitate Dei* as marking the definitive intellectual victory over paganism, see Cochrane, *Christianity and Classical Culture*; and especially Gigon, "Die
abschliessende Replik des Christentums: Augustin's Civitas Dei," in *Die antike Kultur,*
127–141. Consciousness of participation in this worldwide conversion to the Hebrew
God in the Church founded by His Eternal Son Incarnate animates Augustine's treatise
on *The First Catechetical Instruction,* where he shows it to be an integral part of the
method of teaching the Faith in the Catechumenate of the Early Church: *De catechizandis rudibus* chaps. 6, 33, 44–45. Christianity is taught as this visible Catholic
Fact standing on the landscape of universal history, the fulfillment of the Hebrew Fact
with its prophetic literature. "The narration is complete," Augustine writes, "when
the beginner is first instructed from the text: *In the beginning God created heaven and
earth,* down to the present period of Church history." ibid., chap. 3 no. 5. Cf. Jean
Danielou, "Il metodo catechistico," in *La catechesi nei primi secoli* (Torino, IT: Elle Di
Ci, 1969), 203–235, and "È un invito ad una vera teologia della storia," ibid., 235.

[19] Augustine, *De doctrina christiana* III, chap. 34 nos. 47–49 (*Corpus Christianorum,*
Series Latina [Turnhout, BE: Brepols, 1962], 32, pp. 106–110).

[20] Ibid., J. F. Shaw trans., in *Nicene and Post-Nicene Fathers* (Grand Rapids, MI: Eerdmans, 1950), 2:570.

be revoked must be considered to be in the order of time, whose Creator and Administrator is God."[21]

Secondly, there is this "order of time" to be considered in itself. The very concept expresses an openness to the God who is the Creator, and therefore the Lord of history. Hence it is a matter which introduces the very heart of the Judeo-Christian understanding of universal history. This order is first visible to the eye of the intellect in the worldwide conversion of the peoples: when natural reason realizes that this fulfills the Hebrew prophets, it dawns that there is an ordered succession in the very stuff of history, a movement in time from the prophets to this Catholic Fact. Someone is doing something in history. His plan is visible in history. Hence He is the Lord of history.

"The things which were related concerning Christ and the Church," Augustine writes, "have come to pass according to their preordained succession."[22] "In following this religion," he tells Romanianus, "our chief concern is with the prophetic history of the dispensation of divine Providence in time—what God has done for the salvation of the human race, renewing and restoring it unto eternal life."[23] Here an intellectual

---

[21] *De doctrina christiana* II, chap. 28, no. 44 (*Corpus Christianorum*, 63); John J. Gavigan, trans., "Christian Instruction," in *Writings of St. Augustine*, (New York: Fathers of the Church, 1947), 4:99–100. For the chief moments in the Christian correlation of the pagan history with the historical books of the Hebrew Scriptures, see J. Quasten, *Patrology*, (Utrecht, NL: Spectrum, 1953), 2:137–140. On the *Chronicles* of Sextus Julius Africanus, see ibid., 163–297. On Hippolytus of Rome and his "Chronicle of World History," see ibid., 176; and 3:311–314, on "The Chronicle" of Eusebius of Caesarea. Jerome translated Eusebius' work into Latin, and Augustine used it when composing book 18 of *De civitate Dei*, his synthetic correlation of the sacred history of the Bible with secular history of the succession of the Empires of Babylon, Persia, Greece, and Rome.

[22] *De fide rerum* 5.8 (*Corpus Christianorum*, 464–465). *De Christo et Ecclesia quae praedicta sunt, ordinata serie cucurrerunt* (*Corpus Christianorum* 46:14); and cf. *De vera religione* 63.80–81: "The mode of order lives in perpetual truth." This concept of an ordered sequence and succession in time is fundamental in Augustine's thinking, and indeed in the Early Church generally, as Cullmann brings into view in his *Christ and Time: The Primitive Christian Conception of Time and History* (Philadelphia: The Westminster Press, 1950); cf. Patterson, *God and History*. This is the special significance of Augustine's early philosophical dialogue at Cassiciacum, the *De ordine* (*Corpus Christianorum* 29:87–137). For the manner in which Augustine correlated in this dialogue the order of studies with the order in history, indeed with the concretely visible order of things which is bringing the Catholic Fact into historical reality, see E. Kevane, *Augustine the Educator* (Westminster, MD: The Newman Press, 1964), esp. 99–102.

[23] *De vera religione* 6.13 (*Corpus Christianorum*, 196): "Historia et prophetia dispensationis temporalis divinae providentiae pro salute generis humani in aeternam vitam

well-versed in the *historia* of the pagan culture recognizes the historical writings of the Hebrews as *historia*: the same in substance and intent, however different in literary mode and genre. Athens and Jerusalem are coming together.

THE ORDERED SUCCESSION

From this religious succession of the Testaments, Augustine, culminating the work of his Christian predecessors, turns to the civic, social, and cultural succession which the pagan historia records, the sequence of the great empires of antiquity. He finds the basis of correlation between the two successions in the Sacred Scriptures themselves. For the Lord of history exercises His rule over both sequences, and is almighty in His power to coordinate them. With Jerome and early Christian thinkers generally, Augustine recognizes Rome as the Fourth Empire foretold in the Book of Daniel, and thus comes to a fundamental insight regarding the meaning of the conversion of the peoples which he and his fellow thinkers are experiencing. It is nothing else than the conversion of the Roman Empire itself to God in the Church. The Christian Rome of Peter and Paul is in the process of succeeding that other, earlier Rome, exercising a wider sway by the Catholic Faith than pagan Rome had been able to subdue with its marching legions. And this mighty fact, raised up high in universal history for all to see, is under the rule and administration of the Lord of history, who determines the order of times and of successions in the temporal order of the empires.

---

reformandi atque reparandi"; Burleigh, trans., *St. Augustine: Of True Religion*, 14. It would be difficult to improve upon this passage as a witness to the manner in which *historia* is now at home in Christian philosophical thought. Cf. *De vera religione* 25.46–47, Augustine's profound meta-temporal intuition which sees the historical reality of Hebrew prophecy and rises to its source, "the one God who rules all things." (Burleigh, trans., *St. Augustine: Of True Religion*, 42); and 27.50 for "the succession of the people devoted to the one God," the two Testaments, the special character of the Christian Era, and "the divisions of the ages." This is the germ of the reflection upon the structured movement of universal history which will develop into maturity in *De civitate Dei.* And cf. *De catechizandis rudibus* 39, which is actually an outline of *De civitate Dei,* showing how a teaching of the meaning and direction of universal history was an essential part of teaching method in the catechumenate of the Early Church. With the Fathers generally, Augustine made use both of the concept of the Six Ages and the concept of the Four Empires when describing the largest stages of the ordered succession of universal history. Cf. Auguste Luneau, *L'histoire du salut chez les Peres de l'Eglise: La doctrine des Ages du Monde* (Paris: Beauchesne, 1964).

This is the concept of the *translatio imperii,* the succession of the empires, which the Fathers of the Church derived from the Scriptures. Regarding the troubling dream of Nebuchadnezzar, Daniel said: "Blessed be the name of God for ever and ever, to whom belong wisdom and might. He changes times and seasons; he removes kings and sets up kings" (Dan 2:20–21). Then came Daniel's moment of truth before the pagan ruler: "After you shall arise another kingdom . . . and yet a third kingdom . . . which shall rule over all the earth. And there shall be a fourth kingdom, strong as iron, . . . it shall break and crush all these. . . . And in the days of those kings the God of heaven will set up a kingdom which shall never be destroyed, nor shall its sovereignty be left to another people. It shall break in pieces all these kingdoms and bring them to an end, and it shall stand for ever" (Dan 2:39–44). "This fourth empire," Jerome writes in his Commentary, "obviously pertains to the Romans. . . . And at the end of all these . . . our Lord and Savior . . . victorious over all these Empires, has become as a great mountain, and has filled the whole earth."[24]

It is this concept which completes the Christian intellectual understanding of the meaning of the Catholic Fact. When Constantine recognized the Catholic Church and began to make it the official cult of the Empire, a process continuing unto completion in the later fourth century, the Second Coming seemed now indefinitely postponed.[25] More superficial Catholic thinkers, including not a few prelates across the fourth century, accepted the conversion of Rome and the consequent Christianized condition of social laws and custom as the Kingdom or City of God on earth. Others, however, and Augustine above all, recognized the imperfect character of the social *metanoia.* When Alaric sacked Rome in AD 410, the pagans took new scandal at the imperial

---

[24] Jerome, *Commentariorum in Danielem Prophetam* (PL 25, 504). See his prologue, ibid., 491–494, for his refutation of Porphyry's evasion of the Prophet Daniel by attempting to deny the authenticity of the book and to show that it merely describes past events, without reference to coming ones. Contemporary postmodern Christian scholarship has much work to do on this point, close as it is to the eye of the intellectual storm on the meaning and direction of history. One thing is certain: empirical scholarship upon the Book of Daniel must lay aside the colored glasses of Modern philosophy as such to see things with the natural and open vision of postmodern metaphysics.

[25] The psychological effect of this delay was reflected in the Roman Missal of the Mass in the Latin Rite, which was largely composed in this period and carried forward into the Tridentine Missal of 1570. Here the expectation of the Second Coming, vividly voiced in the earlier Eastern Rites, almost disappears. In the Vatican II renewal which led to the Roman Missal of 1970, the expectation of the Second Coming is restored powerfully in the texts and prayers of the Mass of the Latin Rite.

policy. The gods who made Rome great have been abandoned by the Christian conversion, they were saying bitterly, and the Christian God is demonstrably powerless to maintain the Roman power and glory.

FROM CHRISTIAN EDUCATION TO CHRISTIAN CULTURE

Augustine recognized the critical character of the question, and his immense treatise on the *City of God* was the result. The conversion of the Roman Empire does indeed fulfill the prophets: the Christians have succeeded, and the Roman emperor is now a member of the Church. The political and social order has an opportunity to share in the Christian renewal. But he does not expect this political and social order to be or to become the final and perfect condition of mankind. There are two cities, built by two loves, and they are intermingled in the present sixth age, despite the conversion of the Roman Empire, until the Second Coming.[26]

To grasp Augustine's thought fully, the *De doctrina christiana,* his treatise on the Christianization of the classical *paideia,* must be correlated with the *De civitate Dei.*[27]

For the Christian Roman Empire, the Christian social order now ready to move forward into times Augustine could not foresee (although he knew their principles), the times of Charlemagne and Edward the Confessor and Innocent III and St. Louis of France, was dependent upon the new Christian *paideia* which was bringing pagan education and culture under the sway of Christ and passing it on as heritage of Christian humanism to the oncoming generations. The classical *paideia* itself was thus converted, to find for itself a new home and mode of action in the Catechumenate of the Catholic Church. It had begun to

---

[26] *De civitate Dei* (PL 41, 13–804); cf. bk. 14, chap. 28: *Fecerunt itaque civitates duas amores duo; terrenam scilicet amor sui usque ad contemptum Dei, coelestem vero amor Dei usque ad contemptum sui.* For his synthetic view of the Five Ages which prepared the present Sixth Age, cf. bk. 18, chap. l; for the fulfillment of the Hebrew prophets in the Christian events of the sixth age, cf. bk. 18, chaps. 27–54. In bk. 19, chap. 22, Augustine sums up both his treatise and this present sketch of historical understanding in the Judeo-Christian culture: *Magnae caecitatis est, adhuc quaerere quis iste sit Deus. Ipse est Deus, cuius Prophetae praedixerunt ista quae cernimus.* The insight abides: these are words which could well have been written in the postmodern decades of the twentieth century.

[27] This is the theme of Kevane, *Augustine the Educator.*

serve the mission of Jesus Christ, the Divine Teacher. All seven of its Arts function now within the Church and help to maintain this spiritualized Roman Empire, this new Christian culture, in being.

Another term for this spiritualized and converted Roman Empire is simply Christendom, denoting by its suffix the sway or kingship of Christ over hearts, minds, social law, popular custom, and over the political order as King of the kings. The Catholic Fact grows mightily after the times of the Fathers who experienced its beginning, and it stands high on the human scene as a luminous landmark on the ordered succession of largest human social entities which the prophets foresaw.[28]

The seventh art, philosophy, is now "Christian philosophy." Does it have a branch called "philosophy of history," which understands this order and succession in time? Is this the discipline, exactly, which projects the intellectual life of the Early Church to the coming generations of the Christian Era? This question remains to be analyzed. But before it can be done, attention must be given to a new and quite different understanding of meaningful succession in history. And then men will face an agonizing question. Is this new and different concept perhaps what the philosophy of history sees?

---

[28] See notes five in chapter one and eleven in chapter three for the manner in which secular historians perceive this historic reality. Ozanam, Newman, Kurth, and other men of the Christian value judgment see it as an integrating part of Isaiah's sign held high above the peoples and nations, the Christian Rome of Sts. Peter and Paul. See Christopher Dawson, "Is the Church too Western to Satisfy the Aspirations of the Modern World?" in Vittorino Veronese, ed., *World Crisis and the Catholic: Studies Published on the Occasion of the Second World Congress for the Lay Apostolate, Rome* (New York: Sheed and Ward, 1958), 166: "It is impossible for us to understand the Church if we regard her as subject to the limitation of human culture. For she is essentially a supernatural organism which transcends human cultures and transforms them to her own ends. As Newman insisted, the Church is not a creed or a philosophy, but an imperial power, a 'counter Kingdom' which occupies ground and claims to rule over those whom this world's governments had once ruled over without a rival." Cf. John Henry Newman, "Inferences of Assent in the Matter of Revealed Religion," in *An Essay in Aid of a Grammar of Assent* (London: Longmans, Green, 1930), 409–492. The perception of this historic reality foretold by the prophets and standing in the Christian Era was basic to Newman's life and work. Cf. J. Richard Quinn, *The Recognition of the True Church according to John Henry Newman* (Washington, DC: Catholic University of America Press, 1954); and especially Charles Journet, "Apostolicity the Ground of Newman's Conversion to Catholicism," in *The Church of the Word Incarnate* (London: Sheed and Ward, 1955), 1:554–559. For Isaiah's sign, Isiah 11:12, see Pope Pius IX, Dogmatic Constitution *Dei Filius*, April 24, 1870, chap. 3; English in John F. Broderick, S.J., *Documents of Vatican Council I* (Collegeville, MD: The Liturgical Press, 1971), 43–46.

4

THE MODERN VIEW
OF HISTORY

PETRARCH, historians commonly agree, was the first to see
history differently.[1] He recognized with St. Augustine that history
is constituted by the succession in time of the largest socially organized
entities on the human scene. But he no longer perceived the same entities: by some shift of perspective, like an optical illusion, both the form
and the content of the entities he saw in his mind's eye were suddenly
quite different. He saw "Classical Antiquity," the cultural achievement
of pagan Greece and Rome, clearly and with enthusiasm for all their
art forms, their literary style, and in particular the beauty of Ciceronian Latin in contrast with the ecclesiastical Latin in common use
around him in the schools of Christendom. He was keenly conscious
of the burgeoning culture of the Italian cities in his own day, for him
a "Modern Age." Then there was the *medium aevum,* the Age between

---

[1] There is a wealth of literature on Petrarch. A good introduction is James Harvey
Robinson, ed., *Petrarch: The First Modern Scholar and Man of Letters* (New York:
Greenwood Press, 1969). "With prophetic insight," Robinson writes, "Petrarch
declared that he stood between two eras" (p. 4). And Aldo S. Bernaldo, *Petrarch,
Scipio and the "Africa"* (Baltimore: Johns Hopkins Press, 1962). For the specific point
under discussion, that Petrarch was the first to see history differently, see Theodor E.
Mommsen, "Petrarch's Conception of the 'Dark Ages,'" in *Medieval and Renaissance
Studies* (Ithaca, NY: Cornell University Press, 1959), 106–129. Mommsen documents
the fact that Petrarch is the originator of the three mental constructs, "Ancient," "Medi-
eval," and "Modem," and "also the father of the concept or attitude which regards the
Middle Ages as the 'Dark Ages,'" (p. 129).

them. Three concepts are born in this fashion and a meaningful succession between them is conceived. Furthermore, the focal point of interest, the "center," is no longer Jesus Christ, with the fact of the Christianized Roman Empire as the supreme social and political order and reality of the interval between the First and the Second Coming: what Augustine had called "the Christian times" resulting from the conversion of the Roman Empire and what Denis the Little had confirmed in his system of reckoning the years of this new Christian Era from the birth of Christ.[2]

From such a beginning, the modern view of history began to grow and to ripen. How did it happen? What was the background?

Ultimately, it is a question of the Christian perception of this world. Augustine, it has been noted, was careful not to identify the City of God with the earthly temporal order which the conversion of Rome had ushered onto the human scene. Gregory the Great seriously considered the times ripe for the final events which lead directly to the Second Coming. There always have been Christians in every epoch of the Christian Era who have perceived the state of affairs on earth in this way. The Christian Roman Empire is essentially a base for the Worldmission, the ongoing effort to carry forth and to announce the original message of Jesus Christ to all the remaining nations. This base is dependent upon the pastoral ministry for its solidity, upon the personal *metanoia* of the succeeding generations of baptized Christians.

DEFICIENT CAUSES

But Augustine's *causae deficientes* are in full operation.[3] The Christian centuries are not perfect. The two cities continue intermingled in them. There were families for whom baptism was a perfunctory social enrollment; the children were not raised in the actual practice of the Catholic Faith. The *metanoia* was not perfect. The Fathers of the Church knew it already.

Then there were the Jews: an entire people continued its own unconverted existence, dispersed throughout the Christian sway. They

---

[2] Augustine, *De vera religione* 3.3 (CCL 32, i88): "Christianis temporibus quaenam religio potissimum tenenda sit et quae ad veritatem ac beatitudinem via, non esse dubitandum."

[3] See Augustine, *De civitate Dei* bk. 12 chap. 7: "Nemo igitur quaerat efficientem causam malae voluntatis: non enim est efficiens, sed deficiens; quia nee ilia effectio est, sed defectio." A superb insight, developed fully in his *De libero arbitrio*.

were a contrary influence affecting the highest level of Christian leadership; if ever they became unfaithful to the principles of the revealed religion which gave them their being, that influence could become an acute problem.

Then there was the problem of Christian leadership at the level of its intellectual formation in what were now called "universities," the schools of Christendom in their developing and ripening form. Christian philosophy and sacred theology were both frequently taught in a routine and even in a decadent manner.

There was a long interregnum at the Holy See in the late thirteenth century: it caused many Christians to sense a malaise in the Christian social order.

Furthermore, the Worldmission had been blocked by the rise of Islam, confining the message to the old Roman West. Kublai Khan requested two hundred scholars from the Holy See to introduce the Christian *paideia,* the Patristic Christianization of the seven liberal arts, into the cultural life of China. The delay in answering him was very long. At last two men set out over the arduous route across Central Asia and one turned back. When Prince Henry the Navigator finally circumvented the Islamic block on the land routes to India and China by opening up the seaways of the planet, the propitious moment was gone for China to become another Catholic people like Ireland or Poland or Hungary. The opportunity to win China for Christ never really knocked again at the door of universal history.

THE NEW HISTORIOGRAPHY

In any case, Petrarch sensed something about Augustine's Christian times. He was not enthused. The Patristic concept of the Christian Era and its meaning did not enlist his intellectual support. He could not see the received division of history into the Six Ages based on the Hebrew Fact, nor the concept of the Four Empires culminating in Rome and passing to the Christians by a true *translatio imperii* under the rule of the Lord of history.

"The hallmark of the new historiographical temper," writes Patrides,

> is to be found in novel schemes of periodization. Their extensive variations are not nearly so important as is the concerted effort itself to formulate and to adopt non-traditional schemes.

One such scheme was proposed impressively early, had clear-cut implications, and exercised a decisive influence upon later historians. Petrarch, its author, located history's most crucial point in the decline of the Roman Empire, thus neatly disavowing the Christian claim that the Incarnation stands as history's central event. . . . The period of Greece and Rome thus became "classical," the age ushered in by the humanists became "modern," while the intervening centuries were termed—not always with consistency—"Middle Ages." All three designations were standardized by the end of the seventeenth century and represented a scheme of periodization in diametric opposition to the Christian division of history into "BC" and "AD."[4]

The humanists of the Renaissance sealed the new understanding of universal history as a succession of these three distinct and self-contained epochs: The "Ancient," meaning classical (pagan) Greece and Rome; the

---

[4] C. A. Patrides, *The Grand Design of God: The Literary Form of the Christian View of History* (London: Routledge and Kegan Paul, 1972), 49. Cf. Aldo S. Bernardo, trans., *Francesco Petrarca: Rerum Familiarium libri I–VII* (Albany, NY: State University of New York Press, 1975), esp. VI, 2, where Petrarch distinguishes two great periods in history, first Roman Antiquity, then the Christian-Barbarian. This does indeed make the "Fall of Rome" the axis of universal history, and does indeed miss the significance of Christian Rome as the continuation of Rome with its values regenerated and renewed according to the concrete educational and cultural procedures in Augustine's *De doctrina christiana*. The new pattern of historical understanding is born when the Renaissance humanists add their own age, feeling and calling it "Modern," contrasting qualitatively with the age preceding, now perceived simply as barbarous. James Harvey Robinson appears correct when he writes, "Carrying ourselves back to the fourteenth century, we shall find that the name of Francesco Petrarca stands for a revolution in European thought. His existence, character, and career constituted in themselves, as has been said of Voltaire, a new and prodigious era." (*Petrarch: The First Modern Scholar*, 10). "The fall of the ancient world 'is perhaps the most important and most interesting problem of universal history,'" writes F. Lot (*The End of the Ancient World*, 172), quoting the German historian Eduard Meyer. And cf. the preface by Henri Berr: "The progress of human organization and the effort of human cooperation were seen to result in empires—the Empires of the East, Alexander's . . . and the Roman Empire, which inherited a thousand-year-old experience and definitely founded the State, while at the same time it absorbed into itself the essence of a civilization in which Hellas and the East were blended. But this mighty Mediterranean Empire, instead of developing along continuous lines, was destined to decline fairly soon and to go under, after violent and unavailing struggles" (ibid., ix). This does indeed represent a different judgment of value, valuing the pagan state of Rome above the coming era of Christian Rome, and setting the stage for a desire that the pagan culture be reborn.

"Medieval," meaning the Christian period extending for a thousand years from the Fall of Rome, variously dated; and the "Modern," their own times, felt to be so utterly different from and superior to the *medium aevum*. The Renaissance was never simply a rebirth of classical antiquity; always "modernity" was also present, as the quarrel between the Ancients and the Moderns demonstrates.[5] As a matter of fact, thanks chiefly to the triumphs of mathematico-physical science, the Moderns gradually won the victory, so that the Renaissance came to be simply the earlier part of the Modern Age as a whole. [6]

THE ADVENT OF MODERN PHILOSOPHY

Philosophy, the seventh of the seven arts, is the one which gives the first six their orientation and character. Hence, from the viewpoint of education and culture, of the Christianized *paideia,* the most fundamental single intellectual event in the development of the Modern Age was the birth of a new kind of philosophy, replacing Christian philosophy on the level of higher education. This is the significance of Descartes, commonly recognized as the Father of Modern Philosophy. It would be difficult to overemphasize the contrast, for he actually substituted the new mathematical physics for Metaphysics, "the science of wisdom and virtue" as Augustine termed it, which had been cultivated in the schools of Christendom across the centuries since classical antiquity.

Anything which had been so cultivated was now called "scholasticism," a term of opprobrium sharing the common intellectual attitude

---

[5] See Hippolyte Rigault, *Histoire de la querelle des anciens et des modernes* (Paris: Hachette, 1856); and Paul Hazard, *European Thought in the Eighteenth Century: From Montesquieu to Lessing* (London: Hollis and Carter).

[6] Some landmarks in this process include Francis Bacon with his *Novum Organon,* the proliferation of the natural sciences, and Herbert Spencer's question in his educational treatise entitled *What Knowledge Is of Most Worth?* The process leads to the practical disappearance of the classical languages from the education of youth across the closing decades of the nineteenth century. In practice, the humanists have been unable to preserve their Greek and their Ciceronian Latin. In the twentieth century this phenomenon affects even the Catholic Church herself, when in her later decades Ecclesiastical Latin, the mother tongue of the priesthood, tends to disappear not only from liturgical worship but also from the education of young men to the priesthood. This is a phenomenon which may bear some kind of relationship, one which needs further research and analysis, to another *translatio imperii*, and which will be considered further below.

toward the "Middle Ages" which was ripening across the centuries of the Modern Age.

But since Metaphysics is the natural science of intelligible reality first underneath and then beyond the phenomena of this cosmos, the natural science of God the Creator, this philosophical substitution has fateful consequences for education and culture. For mathematical physics, in itself, has no way of knowing any order of reality beyond the phenomena of this cosmos. The consequences will take time to emerge in their logic; but when they do, a qualitative character attaching to Modernity as such will come into view which perhaps will prove to be significant for the philosophy of history. For this qualitative character will be the reverse side of Modern philosophy, the rise and spread of Modern atheism with Spinoza as its metaphysician.[7] It is clear that this view of the world sees cosmic matter as the supreme and eternally abiding reality, and that God the Creator and Lord of history is eliminated from intellectual life.

With this kind of philosophizing ripening in the colleges and universities of higher education, it is obvious that the Judeo-Christian understanding of history will encounter increasing difficulty. During the four centuries between Petrarch and Voltaire, the two understandings, the "Judeo-Christian" and the "Modern," are intermingled, each having its exponents and its treatises. Bossuet published his *Discours sur l'histoire universelle* full in the pattern of St. Augustine only a few years before Voltaire came on the scene. But while catechetical teaching proceeded everywhere in Christendom in terms of historical revelation and saw salvation history as extending to the present times of the Church,[8] higher education, the cultivation of the seven arts, and especially of the seventh, philosophy, turned more and more toward that historical atheism which philosophical atheism logically implies and must therefore necessarily beget. Jean Bodin wrote his impassioned attack on the

---

[7] See the comprehensive treatise of Cornelio Fabro, *Introduzione all'ateismo moderno*, 2nd ed. (Rome: Studium, 1964; 1969); English translation by Arthur Gibson entitled *God in Exile* (New York: Newman Press, 1970). Fabro's analysis culminates in "The virtual atheism of the principle of immanence," (921–945). Fabro's research clarifies the fact that Modern philosophy is an "essence," a particular kind of philosophy with a demonstrable beginning and nature; and that the nature or meaning of Modern philosophy, becoming ever more explicit as its seminal thinkers proceed from the Cartesian beginnings to Kant and beyond, is the rise and spread of modern secularism and atheism. Also Georg Siegmund, *God on Trial: A Brief History of Atheism* (New York: Desclee, 1967). And James Collins, *God in Modern Philosophy* (Chicago: Regnery, 1959), esp. 268–284: "American Naturalism as a Methodological Atheism."

[8] See Augustine, *The First Catechetical Instruction*.

very concept of the Four Empires and their meaningful succession.[9] Boyle published the seminal Encyclopedia in historical atheism. Richard Simon began to introduce this specifically "Modern" type of philosophical and historical thinking into the study of the Bible itself, initiating a type of Scripture scholarship perhaps best denoted by the phrase "purely rational exegesis," that will have its career and its ripening.[10]

Thus the tide rose in higher education against the Judeo-Christian understanding. The "Modern" view seemed ever more self-evident, the inescapable truth of the educated man. There is no personal Supreme Being. At most, there is only the *Deus sive natura* of Spinoza. Therefore, the prophets do not communicate a Word of God.

Consequently, some explaining and interpreting must be accomplished in the case of Jesus Christ by understanding the historical writings of the Judeo-Christian tradition in a new way. Hence the conversion of the peoples to the Catholic Church is not a work of God standing high and beautiful as a great city on the human scene, but rather the beginning of an unfortunate interlude in between, lasting a thousand years, which is better either passed over in silence, or if one is so disposed, exposed and attacked as an unrelieved interval of darkness, ignorance, and superstition.

In other words, the development of Modern philosophy seemed to confirm unto self-evidence the Modern understanding of history as a different kind of succession: that of the Ancient, the Medieval, and the Modern Ages conceived as distinct and self-contained entities. The self-evidence seemed to become apodictic when Fontenelle and Diderot,

---

[9] See John Bodin, "Refutation of Those Who Postulate Four Monarchies and the Golden Age," in *Method for the Easy Comprehension of History* (New York: Columbia University Press, 1945), 291–302. See C.A. Patrides, *The Grand Design of God*, 47–48, 67n67, for references on the attack upon and defense of the Four Empires. Patrides observes accurately that "the secularization of history" is in process: "Such developments signal the abandonment of the providential view of history" (58). And Raymond Aron, *Introduction to the Philosophy of History: An Essay on the Limits of Historical Objectivity* (Boston: Beacon Press, 1961), 258: "It is vain to ask whether history has an end, since Providence is no longer believed in."

[10] See Paul Hazard, "Richard Simon and Biblical Exegesis," in *The Crisis of the European Mind: 1680–1715* (London: Hollis and Carter, 1953), 180–197: "A critic . . . Spinoza certainly was, and one can hardly fail to see in him the direct forerunner of Richard Simon" (184). The phrase "purely rational exegesis" is from the encyclical *Humani generis* of Pope Pius XII, AAS 42 (1950), 561–578. Cf. the translation and comprehensive notes by A. C. Cotter, S.J., *The Encyclical "Humani Generis" with a Commentary* (Weston, MA: Weston College Press, 1951).

at the head of many lesser lights, attached a particular interpretation to the burgeoning and successful mathematico-physical sciences and their applications in technology. The meaning of modern science and technology, they asserted, is simply atheism. Atheism *is* the meaning! If anyone cannot as yet bear psychologically an outright philosophical atheism, let him have recourse to one of its disguises, pantheism or deism; but as to history, historical atheism has become a self-evidence and is incumbent upon all educated men.[11]

THE VOLTAIREAN PHILOSOPHY OF HISTORY

Voltaire comes upon a stage set for him. "You wish that ancient history had been written by philosophers," he writes, "because you are desirous of reading it as a philosopher, *en philosophe.* You seek for nothing but useful truths, and you say you have scarce found anything but useless errors. Let us endeavor mutually to enlighten one another."[12]

With Voltaire, the "Modern" understanding of history wins the victory over the Judeo-Christian, and the Middle Ages become confirmed as simply an interlude of darkness and superstition, the phrase of Edward Gibbon in his work *The Decline and Fall of the Roman Empire,* written in discipleship to Voltaire.[13] Both were filled with feeling against

---

[11] See Paul Hazard, "The City of Men," in *European Thought in the Eighteenth Century,* 113–276; and especially his chapters on "The Encyclopedia," (199–214), and "Diderot," (378–390). This is the taproot of the situation called "The Reality of the Problem," the title of Part One of the *General Catechetical Directory* published by the Holy See (Washington, DC: Sacred Congregation for the Clergy, 1971), nos. 1–9.

[12] Francois Marie Voltaire, *The Philosophy of History* (London, 1766; New York: Philosophical Library, 1965). This work became in later editions the lengthy introduction to his *Essai sur les moeurs et l'esprit des nations,* his rewriting of universal history done to refute Bossuet, open before him as he worked, and in the larger perspective to refute the entire Judeo-Christian intellectual heritage. To emphasize this, and to underline his historical atheism, he begins his survey with China, a people quite devoid of any concept of a revelation from a personal God, and sets the Hebrews aside as later and relatively unimportant. Cf. I. H. Brumfitt, *Voltaire: Historian* (London: Oxford University Press, 1958), esp. chap. 2, "Voltaire and his Predecessors," (26–45), and chap. 5, "The Philosophy of History," (95–128).

[13] See Edward Gibbon, *The Decline and Fall of the Roman Empire* (New York: The Modern Library, 1932), 1:180–476, 2:476–1461. The practical effect upon education in the English-speaking world has been a tendency simply to pass over the period from 476 to 1492 in the syllabi as if there really were nothing there. A professor in my youth

Jesus Christ and the times when He ruled the minds and hearts of men in and through His Church. *Ecrasez l'infame!* The infamous thing which was to be crushed and eliminated from influence upon society was quite simply for them the Catholic Church; and in the century after Voltaire, for their more logical intellectual descendants and followers, the object of the attack was religion in any form.

Is "philosophy of history," then, the invention of Voltaire? It is a common admission among scholars.[14] Certainly he brought the phrase into common use, as the title of his treatise bears witness. Whether his meaning for the word philosophy and his application of the concept to history are legitimate and able to bear analysis is another question.

Beyond doubt, however, Voltaire sealed the victory of the "Modern" understanding of history on the campuses of Western higher education, and passed on to the coming nineteenth century the task of elaborating its meaning and of applying this meaning to programs of political and social action. For the nineteenth century will be the great age of ideological "philosophies of history"—those of Hegel, Marx, Lenin, and Comte, to name only the greater and more socially triumphant ones—all in the Voltairean pattern and each a function of the "Modern" understanding of universal history in the now fixed and "self-evident" categories of "Ancient," "Medieval," and "Modern." Each is accordingly an intellectual and social movement against Him who is the Lord of history in the understanding which has been by now generally replaced in the intellectual life proceeding from the institutions of higher education in the West.

THE TRIUMPH OF SECULAR HUMANISM

It is difficult to exaggerate the completeness of the Voltairean victory across the nineteenth century up to the fateful year of 1914. It was an intellectual victory that was rapidly becoming also a social one. For all

---

advised: "You must make up the deficiency by your own reading. But Gibbon is a waste of time because of his slant. Read the newer scholarship which is rediscovering the positive values of the Christian centuries."

[14] See, for example, Ernst Troeltsch, "Der moderne Ursprung der Geschichtsphilosophie" in *Der Historismus und seine Probleme* (1922; Darmstadt, DE: Scientia Aalen, 1961), 11–27: "The Philosophy of History is a modern creation, a child of the Eighteenth Century," (11); and Friedrich Meinecke, "Voltaire," in *Historism: The Rise of a New Historical Outlook* (New York: Herder and Herder, 1972), 54–89.

social welfare, the advent of a new and perfect society, and even the creation of a "New Man," were conceived to be the function of departure from the influence of the Middle Ages and entry into that of Modernity, with its contrasting man-centered and scientific kind of culture. In the study of this phenomenon of historical understanding, one cannot forget that social welfare, the building of the better world, is attached directly to the atheistic mode of philosophical and hence of historical thought.

The concept "Modern," in the three entities conceived to exist and to succeed in time, has ripened in the period extending from Petrarch to Voltaire. One way or another, in Comte's way of positivism or in that of Marx's and Lenin's Communism, the intellectual life of the nineteenth century was certain of its Modernity: it was absolutely certain that its science and philosophy gave it the keys to social welfare and the tools for building that better world, that City of Man, which had been, since Petrarch, the meaning of the contrast with and the departure from the "Middle Age."[15]

CHRIST ON TRIAL

The French historian Paul Hazard puts it graphically:

> "What had the long process of [Christian] time resulted in?" they asked in a mounting flood of scholarly and popular publication; "Disaster." Why, they asked, was this? Thereupon, they openly professed a charge the like of which for sheer audacity had never before been heard of. Now, the culprit was dragged into open court, and behold, the culprit was Christ! It was more than a reformation that the eighteenth century demanded, it was the

---

[15] To get the "feel" of Western higher education across the decades of the nineteenth century to 1914, see the works of Raissa Maritain, esp. *We Have Been Friends Together* (New York: Doubleday, 1961), where the atmosphere is documented which impacted upon her and Jacques as young students at the University of Paris. The "Modern" weltanschauung, fed by Modern philosophy, was becoming a new "common sense" hardening in all the branches and disciplines of higher education. This "common sense" is quite different from that of natural human thought and discourse, the common sense in which "the natural metaphysics of mankind," in the luminous phrase of Paul VI, has its roots. This situation, which needs much research and analysis, is the substrate of the phenomenon of Religious Modernism, which will be considered briefly below.

total overthrow of the Cross, the utter repudiation of the belief that man had ever received a direct communication from God; of the belief, in other words, in Revelation. What the critics were determined to destroy was the religious interpretation of life. That is why we call Part I of our work "Christianity on Trial."[16]

This points up dramatically to the fact that the understanding of the meaning and direction of history as the succession in time of the three self-contained epoch-entities, "Ancient," "Medieval," and "Modern," was essentially against Christ in His Body, which is the universal Church to which the peoples of antiquity had turned. For Modern philosophy, ripening in a way that Petrarch personally did not foresee nor apparently even desire, generated in the decades from Voltaire through Comte and Marx up to the fateful year of 1914 a new Religion of Progress, a religion without God, a philosophical faith that seemed to be a self-evidence in the intellectual life of the time.[17]

---

[16] Paul Hazard, "Preface," in *European Thought in the Eighteenth Century*, xviii. See also Part One, "Christianity on Trial," 1–110: "It was God, God Himself, who was the prisoner at the bar; the God of the Protestants and the God of the Catholics" (46). This volume of Hazard, member of the French Academy, together with its companion, *The Crisis of the European Mind*, offers a detailed and scholarly study of the ripening of the qualitative mentality of "Modernity" as such. In the latter work, see Part One, chap. 2, "The Old Order Changeth," (29–52), on the quarrel between the Ancients and the Moderns, the shift of emphasis within the modern age from a renaissance of classical antiquity to an increasingly future-oriented interest in and concern for the New Man and his Better World, under construction and soon to be completed.

[17] See Petrarch's letter to Giovanni Colonna, O.P., in Aldo S. Bernardo trans., *Rerun familiarium I–V II* (Albany: State University of New York Press, 1975), 290–291:

> In short, let us philosophize in a manner which the very name of philosophy suggests, for the love of wisdom. Indeed, the true wisdom of God is Christ, so that in order to philosophize rightly we must first love and cherish Him. Let us be such in all things that above all things we may be Christians. Let us thus read philosophical, poetic or historical writings so that the Gospel of Christ resounds always in the ear of our heart. With it alone are we sufficiently happy and learned; without it no matter how much we learn we become ignorant and more wretched. To it all things must be referred as if to the loftiest stronghold of the truth.

"The personal orthodoxy of philosophers and theologians," writes Maritain, "does not suffice, one knows only too well, to guarantee soundness of doctrines, for they have their own proper life and their own logic" (*Revue de Philosophie* [1923]: 500). The understanding of history in the Modern Age has had its own life and logic. "The religious understanding of history," writes Fritz Kern, "as the Prophet Amos, Augustine

But the very mention of 1914, and World War I which it introduces, brings the Voltairean philosophy of history abruptly into a new
situation, one which leaves it historically dated, and which reveals it as
intellectually untenable.

---

and others developed it, has not completely died out in our days. It is being renewed
in distinguished fashion, for example, by the Philosopher of History Christopher
Dawson. Nevertheless, other currents of thought have been more *powerful—und la
faute en est á Voltaire, wie man in Frankreich sagt.* Since the century of the Enlighten-
ment the earlier Christian consensus has been broken" (*Historia Mundi*, vol. 1 [Bern,
CH: Francke Verlag, 1952], 11).

5

THE EMERGENCE OF
POSTMODERN THINKING

THE fact that a different kind of thinking has been growing gradually in the twentieth century, bearing witness to the dated character of Modernity and its view of history, can be documented richly, for it is actually the function of a many-sided scientific progress. It is the fallout from the contemporary knowledge explosion. Only the chief areas can be outlined here, with an almost random indication of works which introduce the inquiring mind into this new intellectual situation.

THE END OF THE MODERN AGE

The concept "Postmodern" seems to have dawned first, fittingly enough, in the mind of a philosopher experiencing the anguish of World War I. The philosopher was Nicholas Berdyaev. "The academical division of history into three parts, ancient, medieval and modern," he writes,

> will soon become obsolete and will be banished from the textbooks. Contemporary history is being wound up. An unknown era is upon us, and it must be given a name. The old measures of history are no longer serviceable, as we realized with a sudden shock when the World War broke out.... The rhythm of history is changing: it is becoming catastrophic.... We are entering ... this new era joylessly and without much hope. We can no longer

believe in the theories of progress which deceived the minds of
the nineteenth century and made the near future seem always
to be better, more beautiful, and more desirable than what had
gone before. . . . What is the explanation of this crisis of European civilization? . . . Modern history, now coming to an end,
was conceived at the time of the Renaissance. *We are witnessing
the end of the Renaissance.*[1]

Forty years later the concept "Postmodern" was no longer philosophically new. The Jewish thinker Will Herberg discusses Berdyaev and
Maritain among others as "heralds of the postmodern mind, trailblazers
in the great, if not always definable, movement of thought that is striv-
ing to go beyond the confident positivism, naturalism, and scientism
that are the hallmarks of modernity"; and he speaks of "the metaphysical
hunger that cannot be stilled with the dry husks of nineteenth-century
platitudes."[2] But the beginnings in philosophy antedated the external
social catastrophe of World War I and its definitive termination of the
Religion of Progress and its "philosophical faith." Edmund Husserl,
for example, was already postmodern in 1900 when he first published
Logishe Untersuchungen (Logical Investigations), his devastating critique of positivism and empiricism, the very heart of the philosophizing
which had been characteristic of the Modern Age as such.[3]

---

[1]   Nicholas Berdyaev, *The End of Our Time* (New York: Sheed and Ward, 1933), 11–13,
his emphasis. The Russian original, published in 1919, was substantially written in the
depths of the Great War: cf. his later work, *The Fate of Man in the Modern World* (Ann
Arbor: University of Michigan Press, 1935), 7.

[2]   Will Herberg, *Four Existentialist Theologians* (New York: Doubleday, 1958), 27. One
is reminded of Peter Wust's classic work in post-World War I Germany, *Die Auferste-
hung der Metaphysik,* on the resurrection of metaphysics. From a different point of
view, but bearing witness to the same insight, cf. William Ernest Hocking, "Passage
Beyond Modernity," in *The Coming World Civilization* (New York: Harper, 1956),
21–42. Likewise Romano Guardini, *The End of the Modern World* (New York: Sheed
and Ward, 1956), esp. chap. 3, "The Dissolution of the Modern World and the World
which is to Come," 68–133. Pondering "the ominous spectacle of a human nature
withering beneath the destructive hand of modernity," Guardini writes: "Our concern
of the moment is neither to repudiate nor to glorify; it is to understand the modern
world, to comprehend why it is coming to an end" (69).

[3]   See the English translation *Logical Investigations,* 2 vols. (London: Routledge and
Kegan Paul, 1970); and his "Philosophy and the Crisis of European Man," in *Phenom-
enology and the Crisis of Philosophy* (New York: Harper Torchbooks, 1965), 149–192.
The fact that he had Edith Stein and Dietrich von Hildebrand as his students and
disciples underlines the postmodern character of Husserl's fundamental thinking.

It may be taken, then, that philosophers have been recognizing the end of Modernity as a living and viable intellectual position. From within the field and curricular discipline of philosophy, the historical category called "Modern" since Petrarch has been placed in philosophical doubt of itself. Meanwhile, the research of truth in other disciplines, some of them entirely new in the last century or so, has been working havoc with all three of the categories: "Ancient," "Medieval," and "Modern."

THE NEW HISTORY

History itself, to begin with, has made a veritable quantum leap forward during the past century, as new techniques for documentation have been discovered and developed. One need only mention names like Von Ranke and Lord Acton. The cumulative effect of this newer scholarship has been to unsettle the category "Medieval," in its pattern of qualifying notes fixed finally by Voltaire, and the category "Renaissance" as the essence of Modernity, fixed similarly by Burckhardt. One scholarly study after another has made it clear that there were other "Renaissances," that of the twelfth Century, and the "Carolingian Renaissance." Has there been simply one long "Renaissance" in successive waves since St. Justin Martyr and Augustine's *De doctrina christiana*? Meticulous scholarship, furthermore, began to reveal a demonstrable cultural continuity from classical antiquity to the Christian culture that succeeded it.[4] Both the beginning and the end of the so-called "Middle Ages" were thus thrown into flux. The newer view of the world-historical importance of Islam linked with the work of Jacques Pirenne cast doubt upon the fall of Rome as the cardinal event of universal history.

Historians themselves, then, apart from the contributions of other disciplines, have been breaking up the neatly self-contained categories of "Ancient," "Medieval," and "Modern," and raising the question of whether they were, after all, only philosophical constructs, intellectually pro-vincial, limited to the subjective impression of one particular cultural moment. For the idea of an historical period, like a sealed compartment, is the sure sign of a philosophical construct. "Western historiography," writes Castellan, "structured its methodological categories prior to

---

4   For a pioneering study on this point, see Alfons Dopsch, *The Economic and Social Foundations of European Civilization* (London: Kegan Paul, 1937).

the great advances made by historical erudition across the nineteenth century."[5]

PREHISTORY

The science of archaeology, an entirely new discovery and development during the two contemporary centuries, has unsettled the category "Ancient" in a similar way. Modernity viewed classical antiquity as a self-contained ideological entity: the pagan culture of Greece and Rome, with its artistic and philosophical forms, and the classical languages as the hallmark of higher education and humanistic culture. Archaeology has broken antiquity open to the rear, revealing a succession of older cultures as the background of the Graeco-Roman world, to which it was affiliated. Furthermore, it was discovered that there was a "Dawn of History" at about 4000 BC, marked by the invention of writing and hence by written records available for scholars today to decipher and to study. But archaeological evidence is not limited, as is history in the strict sense, to these documents: it has been able to penetrate back into a relatively long and hitherto hardly recognized period called the pre-historic past of mankind. Oral traditions, such as those preserved for example in the first book of the Bible and in the writings of Homer, give some insight into these dim times when mankind was dispersed thinly over the earth, prior to the first cities, in family groups organized into tribes or small farming villages.

But the new science of Archaeology, with its excavations of these inhabited sites, has thrown a ray of new light upon this prehistory and revealed the fact that the first cities and their archaic culture, growing naturally and gradually out of these villages, formed the basis for the larger empires of Babylon, Persia, Greece, and Rome which were to come.

Cultural succession and cultural diffusion thus became established as the newer pattern of historical understanding, which had little in common with the limited view of Classical Antiquity which prevailed from Petrarch through Voltaire as its idea of the first of the largest enti-ties of historical succession.[6]

---

[5] Angel A. Castellan, *Filosofía de la historia e historiografía* (Buenos Aires: Dedalo, 1961), 16.

[6] The eminent German scholar Fritz Kern notes the change in perspective: "Two human lifetimes ago Leopold von Ranke began his World History with the Pyramids. Since

THE COMPARATIVE
STUDY OF CULTURES

This same contemporary period, furthermore, has witnessed the rise of the new human sciences of Ethnology, Anthropology, and the Comparative Study of Civilizations. The raw material studied by these disciplines has resulted from the immense outgoing effort of the West to reach all the other peoples of this planet. The origin of this effort, so uniquely characteristic of the cluster of peoples called the Christian West, was simply missionary in character, rooted in the command, "Go therefore and make disciples of all nations, . . . teaching them to observe all that I have commanded you . . ." (Mt 28:19–29). That this has remained fundamentally the mission of the Western expansion in the Modern Age is a fact that comes home when the motivation of Prince Henry the Navigator is studied. For he conceived the conquest of the oceans, which he spearheaded, in the context of the Christian Worldmission, always seeking to bypass the Islamic roadblock and to reach India and China with the message and doctrine of Jesus Christ. After Henry, of course, the mercantile trader began more and more to accompany and then to replace the missionary.

As the base for the Worldmission in the West became an increasingly secularized culture, so the outgoing movement became increasingly one of mere this-worldly imperialism. Yet the Christian effort as such continued deep into the twentieth century, alongside of the secularization, and despite the internal disunity which had come to characterize the missionary enterprise, confusing the populations of Africa and Asia, and blunting the effectiveness of the message.

From the viewpoint of scholarship, the contact of the West with the rest of the world after the conquest of the oceans made available an immense mass of new data regarding the other ways of life on earth:

---

his time Archeology, Ethnology, Racial History, and Genetic Biology have extended our knowledge far earlier. In 1931 Menghin was able to publish his *World History of the Stone Age,* after Schmidt and Koppers in 1924 ventured the first ethnological synthesis of Prehistory" (*Der Beginn der Weltgeschichte* [Bern: Francke Verlag, 1953], 9). For a general overview of the development of the new discipline, see Glyn E. Daniel, *A Hundred Years of Archaeology* (London: Duckworth, 1950); and the now-classic work of William F. Albright, *From the Stone Age to Christianity: Monotheism and the Historical Process* (New York: Doubleday Anchor Books, 1957), esp. chap. 2, "Toward an Organismic Philosophy of History," 82–126, postmodern in its rejection of the Comtean idea that the pattern of succession (Augustine would say the *ordo)* is "given" as the facts are given to historical science.

the more isolated tribal patterns and the great historic civilizations of China, India, and Islam. Thus a new university discipline, the comparative study of cultures, began to emerge, acquire right of place on programs of study, and do its scholarly publishing. And out of this new knowledge Arnold Toynbee proceeded with his vast project for the rewriting of history from this new point of view.[7] Universal history now appeared as a long succession of cultures in time, related to each other in ways scholars were coming increasingly to recognize. Laterally in planetary space the relationship is that of cultural diffusion; longitudinally in historical time Toynbee terms it affiliation.

The particular affiliation between cultures that looms largest in Toynbee's *Study of History* is that between the classical cultures of Greece and Rome, and the Christian culture which followed it. "In short," he writes,

> during the time when the Empire and the Church coexisted as occupants of the same field, the Empire was dead-alive while the Church was animated by a fresh vitality. And so, when the moribund Empire fell, the ensuing "interregnum" gave the living Church an opportunity to perform an act of creation. The Church then played the part of a chrysalis out of which there emerged in the fullness of time a new society of the same species as the old society which had disappeared—but disappeared without carrying away the Church in its ruins as it had carried away the Empire. Thus the Catholic Church was . . . the chrysalis of a new society in gestation. These . . . two societies— the Hellenic and the Western—stood to one another in the relation which we have called Apparentation-and-Affiliation.[8]

It is clear that the fall of Rome, as a hard and fast line of demarcation between "Antiquity" and "The Middle Ages" as Modernity through Voltaire and Gibbon had conceived it, had become untenable and outmoded. At the same time, the Christian culture that succeeded Rome no longer looked like a bleak and empty period of a thousand years best passed over in silence, but rather as the seminal period for the characteristic values of Western Civilization as such. In fact, Toynbee recognizes

---

7 Arnold J. Toynbee, *A Study of History*, vols. 1–10 (London: Oxford University Press, 1934–1954).
8 Ibid., 1:56–57.

suo modo the uniqueness of Jesus Christ and the special presence of the Christian culture which was built into universal history on the basis of His teaching and example.[9] By means of them, continued by the apostolate of the Church He sent to teach in His name, Jesus Christ exercised a sway over minds, laws, home life, social customs, and political policies not unlike that of other examples of merely human emperors or kings of kings, with the exception that His sway was far more deeply rooted in intellectual culture and in the principles of religious and family life, and far more tenaciously lasting than other empires had been. In the newer historiography, therefore, this fact of Christendom in the millennium after pagan Rome has an altogether different meaning and significance than that given to "the Middle Ages" in the older Voltairean construct. It is an integral part of the succession of civilizations, the largest entities of human organization on the planetary scene.[10]

"The place of Christendom in that period of world history," writes the Polish historian Oscar Halecki, "seems absolutely secure and makes that Christendom a clearly distinct field of study in itself."[11] "There is no decisive turning point," he continues, "which could serve as a boundary between ancient and medieval times as far as the Mediterranean region is concerned. More important is the recently stressed issue of the gradual passing from the Mediterranean to the European community. But what seems definitely established is the 'making' of European culture in the course of the first millennium AD, a process which was completed not later than in the tenth century. The realization of the importance of that century is one of the most valuable results of contemporary research in the field of European history."[12]

---

[9] See ibid., 6:175–278, and "Christus Patiens," 6:376–539. It is well known that the insight reached on p. 278 did not continue in its logic, and did not come to its maturity in the later volumes of Toynbee's *Study*. The postmodern situation is anything but clean-cut and unambiguous; see below, note twenty-two in chapter five, on Maritain's experience of the twentieth century, and the topic below on the ongoing problem of Religious Modernism.

[10] This amounts to a rediscovery of Christendom, seen now in a positive evaluation that contradicts the older construct in the "Ancient-Medieval-Modern" pattern. Cf. the strictly postmodern work of the Swiss scholar Gonzague de Reynold, *La formation de l'Europe*, 8 vols. (Paris: Plon, 1944–1957), esp. vol. 8, *Le Toit Chrétien.*

[11] Oscar Halecki, "The Place of Christendom in the History of Mankind," *Journal of World History* (April, 1954): 938. Interestingly enough, this is the UNESCO periodical, and Halecki's article was commissioned by Ralph E. Turner, chairman of the Editorial Committee.

[12] Ibid., 937.

Defining Christendom as "a cultural community with a spiritual basis,"[13] Halecki turns to the postmodern, truly contemporary dimensions of the new perception of reality and nature of Christendom. "The question regarding the real place of Christendom in the history of mankind," he writes,

> has thus become the test, as it were, of two conflicting interpretations of history. This is just one more reason for discussion of it in the free world in a spirit of full scholarly objectivity. It is a question which concerns not only the Middle Ages where the existence of Christendom is unquestionable and only its record a matter of controversy. More difficult and more important is the study of that same question in all other periods of European history, including the modern and contemporary period which so frequently are described as if the very conception of Christendom, doomed with the rise of secularism and modern science, had ceased to exist or lost any real sense."[14]

This is obviously a quite different view of historical entities in succession, one which can only be termed Postmodern, one which has left the older "Modern" view of the first half of the Christian Era behind as outmoded by contemporary scholarship. For Christian culture is not denigrated *a priori* in this new perception of things historical, but rather appreciated positively as a great sign or standard held aloft for the peoples of the planet to see. It is not held up before the nations as something physical or even social, like a World Empire in the earlier pre-Christian sense, but rather as an entity in the realm of the human values. It stands high like a mountain made of precious stones, silver, and gold, where the valuables are the values of a truly human culture.[15]

---

[13] Ibid., 947.

[14] Ibid., 949.

[15] An immense and fruitful field for future research, both empirical and philosophical, opens up in this way for younger scholars to pursue. The seminal minds in this area, all of them basically postmodern, include Frederic Ozanam, John Henry Newman, Kenelm Henry Digby, Godfrey Kurth, Gustav Schniirer, and Christopher Dawson. Perhaps the best general introduction is Dawson's *Progress and Religion: An Historical Enquiry* (New York: Sheed and Ward, 1938), together with his *Religion and the Rise of Western Culture* (London: Sheed and Ward, 1950).

THE ADVENT OF
POSTMODERN THINKING

The outbreak of World War I, then, can be taken as a watershed date, symbolizing the manner in which the cumulative effect of the more recent scholarship in the human social and historical sciences has literally demolished the three categories "Ancient," "Medieval," and "Modern." They have been broken apart and reduced to rubble by the explosion of contemporary knowledge.

Philosophers, therefore, are in a position to recognize what these categories were: dated philosophical constructs which resulted from the union of a particular subjective ideological disposition with a limited and parochial view of the historical reality.

It is characteristic of the twentieth century, after 1914, that the postmodern realization dawns gradually upon more and more minds, while the older modern outlook, upon the meaning and direction of historical succession, especially with its view of "the Middle Ages," lingers on only in popular publications, in the rut-like tracks of school textbooks, or where the Voltairean philosophy of history is imposed by certain university in-groups or by raw political power and its techniques for the control of thought.

The advent of postmodern thinking comes home even more forcefully when the twentieth century revolution in the physical sciences is given due consideration. The renaissance of Classical Antiquity was one of the fundamental components of Modernity, and nowhere was this more true than in philosophy itself. The doctrine of creation brings this clearly into view. For the pagan philosophy of pre-Christian times, it will be recalled, was characteristically unable to rise to this insight into the nature of the existence of the visible cosmos. For paganism, matter is eternal. The gods, if there are any, at most shape and form a preexisting stuff.

The Christian philosophy cultivated in the Schools of Christendom from Justin Martyr and Augustine through Aquinas toward Descartes was characterized by a new and far more lucid concept of God as *ipsum esse*, Existence Itself, with all other existing realities participating in existence, each in its own particular and limited way, thanks to the divine act of creation.[16] This insight philosophizes within the Catho-

---

[16] The works of Etienne Gilson, professor at the Sorbonne across the twentieth century, bring the historic reality of Christian philosophy, especially in this its fundamental characteristic, clearly into view; see especially *God and Philosophy* (New Haven, CT:

lic Faith which the Apostles' Creed professes, for whoever calls himself Christian begins his profession with a formally stated Article of Faith: "I believe in God, the Father Almighty, Creator of heaven and earth."

Descartes no longer sees the doctrine of creation clearly; and in his disciple Spinoza, the metaphysician of modern atheism, it disappears entirely. From Spinoza on through the history of Modern philosophy as such, the doctrine of creation is characteristically absent. Philosophers in the pattern of Modernity again conceive of matter in the mode of Classical Antiquity as something eternal, operating mechanically or by chance—or by some immanent *Weltgeist* or *élan vital*, when atheism feels it must wear its pantheistic mask. Such concepts are the very essence of the nineteenth century philosophies of history, especially in the Hegelian and Marxist forms; and always Modern philosophy conceived itself to think and to teach in some kind of pre-established harmony with the meaning of the physical sciences.[17]

SCIENCE DISCOVERS CREATION

All of this came rather abruptly to an end in the same turn from the nineteenth into the twentieth century. The atoms of matter are discovered to be not tiny solid balls but empty space structured like the planetary system. And the new discipline of Astrophysics becomes able to demonstrate that the entire visible cosmos had a beginning. It even calculates approximately how long ago this event took place. Not only that: it also observes that the cosmos is proceeding on a linear course of development that projects toward its mathematically predictable end. During this development, furthermore, the cosmos is ruled by constant laws, non-material in character, that postulate a reality standing outside

---

Yale University Press, 1959); *Christianity and Philosophy* (London: Sheed and Ward, 1939); and *The Spirit of Medieval Philosophy* (New York: Scribner's, 1940), the Gifford Lectures for 1931–1932.

[17] Again a fertile field for fresh thought and liberating research opens for younger scholars. The suspicion is growing among them already that the meaning of science is not atheism, but rather the contrary. The research already is pursuing relentlessly the dated and purely philosophical character of the atheistic mentality, and beginning to separate it rigorously from the sciences. See James Collins, *God in Modern Philosophy* (Chicago: Regnery, 1959); M.F. Sciacca, ed., *Con Dio e contro Dio: Raccolta sistematica degli argomenti pro e contro l'esistenza di Dio*, 2 vols. (Milan: Marzorati, 1972); and especially the works of Philip Dessauer and Adolf Partmann in German.

the space-time continuum, giving it not only its existence in general, but also the modes and kinds of existence that appear as phenomena of the continuum.[18]

In other words, physical science itself suddenly has become postmodern in a philosophical sense: it leaves Modern philosophy behind as an outmoded construct, and, with a new openness to the First Article of the Creed, calls for a mode of philosophizing that bears primarily upon existence as such.[19] Such a philosophy concerned with the act of existing

---

[18] The twentieth century has witnessed the gradual accumulation of works which explain the new science ever more intelligibly to the non-mathematician. Beginning with those of James Jeans, *The Universe Around Us* (Cambridge, UK: Cambridge University Press, 1929) and *The Mysterious Universe* (Cambridge, UK: Cambridge University Press, 1931); and of A.S. Eddington, *The Nature of the Physical World* (Cambridge, UK: Cambridge University Press 1929), one comes by way of mid-century studies such as Sir Edmund Whittaker's, *Space and Spirit* (Chicago: Regnery, 1948), to the more contemporary syntheses which bear witness to the rediscovery of the doctrine of creation by the empirical sciences. See, for example, Henri Bon, *La creation: verite scientifique du XXe siècle* (Paris: Nouvelles Editions Latines, 1954); Pierre Loyer, *Du cosmos a Dieu* (Paris: Nouvelles Editions Latines, 1971); Claude Tresmontant, *Sciences de l'univers et problèmes metaphysiques* (Paris: Éditions du Seuil, 1976). There are many university professors in the United States who teach "Creation Science." See, for example, the Institute for Creation Research, San Diego, CA, and its literature. For a recent example of this unique literature of the twentieth century, see Robert Jastrow, *God and the Astronomers* (New York: W.W. Norton, 1978), a book occasioned by the awarding of the 1978 Nobel Prize to two American physicists for their discovery "by accident" (p. 20) of empirical evidence for the first moment of the existence of this entire visible cosmos. "The astronomical evidence proves that the Universe was created twenty billion years ago in a fiery explosion" (p. 12). Jastrow calls these discoveries "strange developments" which indicate "that the Universe had, in some sense, a beginning—that it began at a certain moment in time" (p. 11). Jastrow's conclusion: "The scientist's pursuit of the past ends in the moment of creation. This is an exceedingly strange development, unexpected by all but theologians. They have always accepted the word of the Bible: In the beginning God created heaven and earth" (p. 115). At the very least, for any student of Modernity as such with its characteristic philosophical resistance to the First Article of the Creed, these developments (expected or unexpected) must be termed postmodern. *Aeterni Patris,* representing metaphysical openness to the doctrine of Creation, can celebrate its centenary with a certain sense of calm intellectual peace.

[19] The new physics calls for the omnipresence of the Supreme Spiritual Power throughout the entire space-time continuum, exercising upon it an ongoing *creatio continuata* without which its laws of being and operation would vanish into nothingness, and with them the continuum itself. The modes of being of course contain factors of temporal development, "evolution" if one wishes to use a word still laden with the inadequate understandings that hold over into the twentieth century from the philosophizing of atheistic Modernity as such. Cf. Loyer, *Du cosmos a Dieu*, 40; Tresmontant, *Sciences*

de l'univers, 14–15, 20–26, where it is recognized that the materialism and atheism of Modernity has simply been "condemned to death" by the discoveries of postmodern science. For a thoroughly postmodern presentation of Christian doctrine, able to see biological evolution, defined with accurate scientific limitation, as a law of the Creator giving a certain portion of His living creation its kinds and its modes and sustaining them in the very being of their seeds and kinds, there is the work of the English priest and priestly philosopher Edward Holloway, *Catholicism: A New Synthesis* (London: Keyway, 1970). The *creatio continuata,* which the inner eye of Christian philosophy has been able to see since its birth in Patristic thought, is receiving a powerful new empirical support in the postmodern situation of mankind. Holloway recognizes lucidly the uniqueness of the human mode of existing, which calls for the special creation of each human being in and with the seminal mode. See especially pp. 82–93. In general, this priestly work in philosophical thought, coming late in the first century of *Aeterni Patris,* merits careful study by those who carry the renewal of Christian philosophy forward into its second century. Etienne Gilson laments in his urbane work *The Philosopher and Theology* (New York: Random House, 1962) that the renewal never yet has come properly to grips with Bergson's effort to break away from the atheistic materialism of Modern philosophy. Father Teilhard de Chardin failed abjectly. Father Holloway intends explicitly to replace the Teilhardian confusion with a work truly sound in metaphysics, truly open to the transcendent God of the Judeo-Christian Revelation, and truly at home with all the findings of the contemporary empirical sciences. Father Holloway himself recognizes that his work is a beginning, not a finished intellectual product. But here one is constrained to mention an apparent defect in the realm of history and the philosophy of history. On the one hand, this work is distinguished by an adequate concept of the all-present active Supreme Being, by a perceptive rejection of the Modernist "New Theology," and by a sustained criticism of the errors of Marxism. On the other hand, especially in the final chapter, "The Scientific Society" (pp. 448–491), it leaves the impression of a pro-Marxist bias in that it praises the coming "one world," "one common civilization of Science," without discerning the concrete reality during Modern times of the Great Apostasy from the divine plan for the Kingship of Christ in world society. Thus Father Holloway does not come to grips with the necessity of conversion on the part of the Wall Street managers of the great worldwide corporations and on the part of the Kremlin managers of the Communist Parties throughout the world. This is to leave matters in a realm of philosophical abstraction open to the unfortunate impression just mentioned. Our Lady, in her maternal visits to this troubled planet beginning in 1830, is always concrete: she gives specific instructions on what each one must do concretely in order that healing events like the conversion of Russia may take place in the temporal order. In other words, Father Holloway's work, so admirable and so priestly in its intention and its substance, so superior to the work of Father Teilhard de Chardin, needs further study by younger Catholic scholars in the second century of *Aeterni Patris* to effect that better coordination of philosophy and theology for which Vatican II calls. He himself is commendably open to this on p. 503 in his final word. This demands a greater attention to the meaning and direction of the concrete realities of actual history, including the factual nature of the apostasy of the once-Christian West. One must ponder the historical character of Revealed Religion, as Newman did in all his life and work. Dom Gregory Dix stated this character well in his *Jew and Greek: A Study in the Primitive Church* (New York: Harper, 1953), 5:

would only secondarily devote itself to the kinds and modes and essences in which particular things exist, as they are observed to be in the cosmos. In Aristotle's time, this latter task was uppermost for the philosopher, reflecting on the data of the unaided senses; but in recent times, due to the articulation and development of the various empirical sciences, together with the new techniques for assisting and amplifying the power of the senses to observe phenomena, this task of studying the kinds and natures of natural substances has become primarily their province.

Is there such a mode of philosophizing? There is, indeed. The Christian philosophy born in the catecheses of the Fathers of the Early Church

---

Christianity is the revelation of Divine Truth from beyond all history and all time, but it is so only because it is the only fully historical religion. It is the only religion which actually *depends entirely upon* history. It is faith in the Incarnate God, it is Divine redemption given from *within history,* not by the promulgation of doctrines (even true doctrines) but by the wrenching of one Man's flesh and the spilling of His blood upon one particular square yard of ground, outside one particular city gate during three particular unrepeatable hours, which could have been measured on a clock. You cannot (and you never could) enter into the truth of Christianity apart from its history. And that historical *condition* of Christian truth is not something which begins at Bethlehem and ends at Olivet. It applies equally to the Church, the Body of Christ, which He launched into history no less unreservedly than the Body of His flesh. (Emphasis in original.)

The St. Augustine of *The First Catechetical Instruction,* with its "From Genesis to the present times of the Church," would accept this historical concreteness. It is the basis for the Christian philosophy of history. The divine plan for the unification of mankind is concretely offered to mankind. If accepted, the Kingship of Christ, with all its benefits for human persons and human rights, will function on this planet. But if it is not accepted, then any coming "one world" will necessarily be an anti-Christian Empire. Christians may see it coming and Christians may live under it, indeed as Christians. But they should not applaud its coming, much less abet its triumph, or even seem to do so. In an age of cunning intellectual deceptions, the apostolate of intellectual clarity will be an increasing need. Younger scholars will be called upon to hammer out the intellectual positions on these matters with all the careful distinctions which minister to clear understanding. The philosophy of history will assist them greatly in their work of coordinating philosophy and theology according to the *Optatam totius* of Vatican II. Indeed, the time may well come when Father Halloway's plea for "unilateral disarmament" (p. 477) will take on a new light if there is to be a worldwide political and social triumph of the atheistic ideology. It would then appear to be the fundamental thinking which underlies a patient and nonviolent suffering of the situation in the spirit of the Early Church. At the same time, it remains true that Vatican II does not espouse "unilateral disarmament" in its call for an ending of the arms race. Cf. Paul VI, Pastoral Constitution on the Church in the Modern World *Gaudium et spes,* Dec. 7, 1965, §82, in Flannery, ed., *Vatican Council II,* 991.

and elaborated in the schools of Christendom produced a metaphysical genius named Thomas Aquinas, who carried the insights of his predecessors on *ipsum esse* and *creatio ex nihilo,* especially those of Augustine, far beyond the level achieved by Plato and Aristotle. He carefully distinguished the essences of things from their acts of existing, the act by which a thing is real, by which it really and actually is. For each concrete thing can be studied first from a viewpoint which asks what kind of essence it is, and here the empirical sciences have taken over in a new way; and secondly, from the viewpoint of its act of existing. How can one understand that it *has* this act, that it *is,* instead of having remained the nothingness that it once was and whence it somehow came?[20]

THE CATHOLIC CHURCH AND PHILOSOPHY

With this, one stands suddenly before the question of whether the Catholic Church has a position in philosophy. And if so, whether it is Modern or Postmodern?

The answer is immediately clear, both from philosophical analysis and from the authority of the Magisterium. The position is stated in the Constitution *Dei Filius* of Vatican I and in the consequent program for the renewal of Christian philosophy in all Catholic institutions of higher education. For the Holy See launched this renewal to imple-

---

[20] In his *Introduction to Metaphysics* (New York: Doubleday, 1959), 1, Martin Heidegger asks, "Why are there essents rather than nothing... why is there anything at all, rather than nothing?" This is to ask the correct question. But Heidegger remains embedded in the philosophizing of the Modern Age as such, never able to break through to the postmodern liberation. It is deeply significant as Tresmontant points out (*Sciences de l'univers,* 14–17, 39–42) that Heidegger and Sartre studiously ignore the evidence of twentieth century empirico-mathematical science for the beginning and the contingency of the *existence* of the cosmos. "The work of Heidegger, and that of Sartre, could have been written . . . in the 4th Century, in the time of Proclus . . ." (15). These Existentialists symbolize the way in which modern philosophizing tends to hold over into the postmodern situation, in a manner that has religious significance and a bearing upon theology which will be discussed below. For Heidegger, it is always *The Question of Being* (New Haven, CT: College and University Press, 1958), never the Answer; the refusal to recognize *Ipsum Esse Subsistens* as *Das Sein;* always *Das Sein* as a *Vorstellen* in man's own mind, and not Yahweh, the Creator of heaven and earth. A man-centrism that is atheism by implication and by silence?

ment Vatican I and has sustained it consistently to the present.[21] The fundamental reason for doing so is pastoral in character. Repeatedly, in document after document, the reason given is this metaphysics of openness to Yahweh, the Hebrew God of creation and revelation, who sent His Eternal Son in whom the Catholic Creed continues its changeless profession.

The entire philosophical program of the Catholic Church from Vatican I, across 1914 and through Vatican II to the present, has been qualitatively Postmodern.[22] This has far-reaching consequences for the philosophy of history, for one must ask next, what kind of thought

---

[21] For *Aeterni Patris* see Etienne Gilson, ed., *The Church Speaks to the Modern World* (New York: Doubleday Image Books, 1954), 31–54. For the important official title of this encyclical, frequently missed in translations, see footnote 4 in the introduction. The Documents of the Holy See which repeatedly confirm this renewal are too numerous to list here. Let one serve as an example of them all: the Address of Pope Paul VI to the Sixth International Thomistic Congress (Rome, Sept. 10, 1965), in *The New Scholasticism* (January 1966): 80–83; it is noteworthy that Paul VI calls this philosophical position "the natural metaphysics of the human intelligence. . . . This permanent value of Thomistic metaphysics explains the attitude of the Magisterium of the Church in its regard" (p. 82). This theme recurs constantly in the philosophical Addresses of Pope Paul VI and it formed the foundation for his ongoing catechetical instructions in his regular meetings with the public as the implicit natural substrate for his fidelity to the Christian message, without the reinterpretation proposed by Modernity as such. Cf., for example, "Faith and History," *L'Osservatore Romano* English Edition (October 7, 1976), 1, 12. The Holy See is abidingly postmodern ever since Vatican I and *Aeterni Patris*. Pope Paul VI reaffirmed luminously the place of St. Thomas Aquinas in this renewal on the occasion of the seventh centenary of the death of St. Thomas Aquinas. See his apostolic letter *Lumen Ecclesiae* (November 20, 1974), in *L'Osservatore Romano* English Edition (January 30, 1975), 6–11. In a strong and lucid move, Pope John Paul II likewise reaffirmed the entire program of *Aeterni Patris* with his apostolic constitution *Sapientia Christiana* (April 15, 1979), AAS 71 (1979), 469–499. In §§71 and 80, on the norms of sound teaching method in theology and philosophy, the pope refers to *Optatam totius* of Vatican II and to this document *Lumen Ecclesiae* of his predecessor Pope Paul VI. The bearing of all this upon the second century of the renewal, about to open, is clear to see.

[22] This fact can be seen and studied perhaps best in the life and work of Jacques Maritain. See, for example, Charles Journet, "D'une philosophie chrétienne d'histoire," *Revue Thomiste* (1948): 33–61, in the special issue, "Jacques Maritain, son oeuvre philosophique." Maritain's philosophical life was a postmodern intellectual struggle with holdover Moderns, anxious to set him aside as a mere *laudator temporis acti* (one who praises past times), who were blind to the principles of a Christendom as distinct from particular temporal realizations, including that relatively large and compact one prior to Petrarch. Cf. Brooke Williams Smith, *Jacques Maritain, Antimodern or Ultramodern?—An Historical Analysis of His Critics, His Thought and His Life* (New York: Elsevier, 1976).

about history takes place in Christian philosophy? Furthermore, does it offer any assistance in evaluating Modern philosophy as such, together with its now-outmoded view of the past as an order or succession of those three particular and restricted constructs, "Ancient," "Medieval," and "Modern"?

6

THE PHILOSOPHY OF HISTORY
IN CHRISTIAN PHILOSOPHY

T HE categories "Ancient," "Medieval," and "Modern," then, stand
revealed as nothing but philosophical constructs. Historical
succession seen in this context falls short of an objectively valid understanding of the order of things human in time. The grandiose and exotic
nineteenth century philosophies of history of Hegel, Comte, and Marx,
elaborated in terms of these categories, have been so discredited intellectually that authors tend to apologize for the very use of the phrase.[1]
Is a philosophy of history possible? Can philosophy as such know the
meaning and direction of history?

THE NATURE OF MODERNITY

The analysis which leads toward the answer has a negative and then a
positive aspect. Negatively, perhaps the best insight into the matter is
provided by Eric Voegelin, a truly postmodern thinker, on the nature
of Modernity. He sees it as a diversion of the Christian understanding
of the end of history into a position within history, as if the meaning
and direction of history were the construction of the kingdom of God

---

[1] See Raymond Aron, *Introduction to the Philosophy of History*, 9: "The title of this book
runs the risk of misleading the reader who might identify the philosophy of history
with the great systems of the beginning of the nineteenth century, so discredited today."

within history. Augustine and Ambrose never meant this when they saw temporal society functioning *suo modo* within the Church and political rulers performing their specific offices as members of the Church.[2]

"Joachim of Flora," writes Voegelin,

> broke with the Augustinian conception of a Christian society when he applied the symbol of the Trinity to the course of history. . . . In his trinitarian eschatology Joachim created the aggregate of symbols which govern the self-interpretation of modern political society to this day. . . . The first of these symbols is the conception of history as a sequence of three ages, of which the third age is intelligibly the final Third Realm. . . . As variations of this symbol are recognizable the humanistic and encyclopedist periodization of history into ancient, medieval and modern history; Turgot's and Comte's theory of a sequence of theological, metaphysical and scientific phases; Hegel's dialectic of the three stages of freedom and self-reflective spiritual fulfillment; the Marxian dialectic of the three states of primitive communism, class society, and final communism; and, finally, the National Socialist symbol of the Third Realm . . .[3]

---

[2]   See L. G. Patterson, *God and History in Early Christian Thought* (London: Black, 1967), 94ff., on the contrast between Sts. Ambrose and Augustine on the one hand, and the Eusebians on the other. "We can now see very easily how naive was the reliance of these fourth-century Christians on the assumption that the events of the time heralded a period of peace and prosperity" (94). Patterson goes so far as to speak of ". . . Augustine's virtual repudiation of the significance of a Christian empire . . ." (152).

[3]   Eric Voegelin, *The New Science of Politics: An Introduction* (Chicago: University of Chicago Press, 1952), 111–112. See in general his chapter 4, "Gnosticism—The Nature of Modernity," 107–132. For Joachim, the three ages in historical succession are those of the Father, under the leadership of Abraham; of the Son, under the leadership of Jesus Christ; and of the Holy Spirit, under the leadership of one still to come, one who will introduce a new kind of religious life and hence a better world. Joachim, who imagined that the Age of Jesus Christ was to end at AD 1260, set a pattern of thinking about forerunners of the coming leader, "paracletic figures," a concept that will emerge in later secularized stages of Modern philosophy as the "Supermen" of Comte, Marx, and Nietzsche. In this pattern of thinking, "the course of history as an intelligible, meaningful whole must be assumed accessible to human knowledge, either through a direct revelation or through speculative gnosis. Hence, the Gnostic prophet, or, in the later stages of secularization, the Gnostic intellectual, becomes an appurtenance of modern civilization. Joachim himself is the first instance of the species." (112). For the broadening and deepening of Voegelin's insight into Gnosticism, see *Order and History*, vol. 4, *The Ecumenic Age* (Baton Rouge: Louisiana State Univ. Press, 1974), 1–58. For Joachim of Flora, see Marjorie Reeves, *The Influence of Prophecy in the*

At the heart of Voegelin's analysis is his perception of Modernity as a rebirth of the ancient Gnosticism in its misconception regarding the nature and power of philosophical thought, its relationship to religious truth, and in particular its overconfident attitude toward the ability of natural reason to know the order of history as such. Thus Modern philosophy, with its characteristic Voltairean, Hegelian, and Marxist concept of the philosophy of history, is a function of the Gnostic replacement of religious faith with philosophical faith. "The attempt at immanentizing the meaning of existence," Voegelin points out, "is fundamentally an attempt at bringing our knowledge of transcendence into a firmer grip than the *cognitio fidei*, the cognition of faith, will afford, and the Gnostic experiences offer this firmer grip insofar as they are an expansion of the soul to the point where God is drawn into the existence of man."[4] And again: "The totalitarianism of our time must be understood as journey's end of the Gnostic search for a civil theology."[5]

Later Middle Ages: A Study in Joachimism (Oxford, UK: Clarendon Press, 1969). For Aquinas' lucid rejection of Joachimism, see S.T., I–II, q. 106, a. 3–4; II–II, q. 174, a. 6; cf. Max Seckler, "Saint Thomas d'Aquin et Joachim de Flore," in *Le salut et l'histoire: la pensee de 5. Thomas d'Aquin sur la theologie de l'histoire* (Paris: Cerf, 1967), 179–185. Gnosticism, while retaining redefined and reinterpreted Christian terminology, always moves against Christ, replacing Him with a new Coming One, and always attempts to subvert the Catholic Church in its original and abiding constitution with a Magisterium and Sacraments. "The Third Age of Joachim," writes Voegelin,

> by virtue of its new descent of the spirit, will transform men into members of the new realm without sacramental mediation of grace. In the Third Age the Church will cease to exist because the charismatic gifts that are necessary for the perfect life will reach men without administration of Sacraments. While Joachim himself conceived the new age concretely as an order of monks, the idea of a community of the spiritually Perfect who can live together without institutional authority was formulated on principle. The idea was capable of infinite variations. It can be traced in various degrees of purity in medieval and Renaissance sects, as well as in the Puritan churches of the saints; in its secularized form it has become a formidable component in the contemporary democratic creed; and it is the dynamic core in the Marxian mysticism of the realm of freedom and the withering away of the state. (112–113)

It is the emptiness of this construct which Solzhenitsyn experienced so keenly and describes so graphically in his works, an emptiness to which the growing volume of *Samizdat* literature bears witness.

[4] Ibid., 124.

[5] Ibid., 163. Again, important perspectives open up to younger scholars for research on Modern philosophy as such, time and culture conditioned as it is and with a demonstrable beginning and ending, as a rebirth of the ancient Gnosticism which troubled the Early Church so deeply. Cf. the bibliographical leads in Voegelin, ibid., 124. Seen

HISTORY NOT AN ESSENCE

Voegelin's analysis reaches its climax in his forthright rejection of the Gnostic attempt to grasp an *eidos* of history. The Gnostic attempt to construct categories of historical understanding out of mere philosophy as such is its characteristic abuse of reason. "The Gnostic fallacy," he writes, "destroys the oldest wisdom of mankind . . . what comes into being will have an end, and the mystery of this stream of being is impenetrable. These are the two great principles governing existence. The Gnostic speculation on the *eidos* of history, however, not only ignores these principles but perverts them into their opposite."[6] Thus "Gnosticism . . . creates a dream world which itself is a social force of the first importance in motivating attitudes and actions of Gnostic masses and their representatives."[7]

History, in other words, when one understands the word to mean the formal object of a discipline called the philosophy of history, is not an "essence," not a "substance." It does not have a "nature" which empirical sciences can observe and categorize, and which philosophical reflection can define. It is rather an order by which such essences and natures succeed each other in time. But this order, *ordo* in Augustine's precise sense, is not itself an *eidos*, an essence.

---

from this point of view, Comte, Marx, and Nietzsche are all nineteenth century Modernist Gnostics, who cast long shadows out of Modernity into postmodern times, shadows which help to explain how Religious Modernism, with its Marxist leanings, can continue to exist and seem alive in the years after 1908 and 1914.

[6]   Ibid., 160–167, with reference to Ecclesiastes (Qoheleth) 3 where man's natural inability to know God's purposes in the order and succession of events in time is explicitly stated.

[7]   Ibid., 167. Voegelin speaks of "Gnostic insanity" (p. 170), and "The pathological substitution of the dream world" (p. 172). If these concepts seem too strong, one must study the fundamental work of Cornelio Fabro, *Introduzione all'Ateismo Moderno*. Fabro's comprehensive analysis of Modern philosophy as such, from Descartes to Nietzsche, Heidegger, Marx and Lenin, reveals its implacable tendency toward atheism, a tendency constituted by its Cartesian, Spinozan, and Kantian immanentism, its turning of human thought down from the personal God of creation and in upon the merely human understood simplistically as an experience of organismic being in time. Fabro and Voegelin taken together, and with them the growing number of postmodern thinkers, establish two facts, each increasingly relevant for the philosophy of history. The first is that Modernity, as a process in history and as a view of history, is "a Gnosticism . . . which is a fall from faith in the Christian sense as a mass phenomenon" (Voegelin, ibid., 123); and the second is a paraphrase of Marx's dictum on religion: atheism is the mental illness of mankind.

"From the Joachitic immanentization," Voegelin writes,

> a theoretical problem arises which occurs neither in classic
> antiquity nor in orthodox Christianity, that is, the problem of
> an eidos in history. . . . There is no eidos of history because
> the eschatological supernature is not a nature in the philosoph-
> ical, immanent sense. The problem of an eidos in history, hence,
> arises only when Christian transcendental fulfillment becomes
> immanentized. Such an immanentist hypostasis of the escha-
> ton, however, is a theoretical fallacy. Things are not things, nor
> do they have essences, by arbitrary declaration. The course of
> history as a whole is no object of experience; history has no
> eidos, because the course of history extends into the unknown
> future. The meaning of history, thus, is an illusion, and this illu-
> sory eidos is created by treating a symbol of faith as if it were a
> proposition concerning an object of immanent experience.[8]

Sifting Voegelin's principle from his terminology on the eschaton as "a
symbol of faith," a valuable insight emerges regarding the origin of the
view of history characteristic of Modernity. The great "philosophies of
history," which it begets from Voltaire across the years to 1914, are the
result of projections from Modern philosophy, as such, onto the matter
of history, creating in it, as it were, a form of understanding of the *ordo,*
the meaning of the succession in time of its largest human entities. This,
however, is exactly what philosophical reason cannot do—no matter
what aid it gets from the other six liberal arts—for the formal object it
seeks to understand, the *ordo successionis* as such, is beyond their facts
and its grasp. Voegelin is correct: Gnostic Modernity is an aberration in
philosophy, one which effects the pathological substitution of an illusion, a dream world, for the contours of reality which men can see if,
turning from subjective constructs of reason wrongly used, they give ear
to the word which has come to this planet through the prophets.

AUGUSTINE'S ANALYSIS

It is becoming clear that postmodern thinking is beginning to use once
again the abiding insights of Christian philosophy as such, in its meta-

---

[8] Ibid., 120.

physical openness to God, the Creator of participated existences and the Administrator of the order of succession of these created beings in time.[9]

It is Augustine himself who stated positively this basic position of the Christian philosophy of history which Voegelin recovers. The Bishop of Hippo rejects the Gnostic aberration in philosophy with its proud self-assurance regarding the ability of reason to discern the origin, meaning, direction, and goal of history. "These persons," Augustine writes,

> promise themselves cleansing by their own righteousness for this reason, because some of them have been able to penetrate with the eye of the mind beyond the whole creature, and to touch, though it be in ever so small a part, the light of unchangeable truth; a thing which they deride many Christians for being not yet able to do, who, in the meantime, live by faith alone. . . . These people also blame us for believing in the resurrection of the flesh, and rather wish us to believe themselves concerning these things. As though, because they have been able to understand the high and unchangeable substance by which the things are made, for this reason they had a claim to be consulted concerning the revolutions of mutable things, or concerning the connected order of the ages, *de contexto saeculorum ordine.* For pray, because they dispute most truly and persuade us by most certain proofs that all things temporal are made after a science that is eternal, are they therefore able to see clearly in the matter of this science itself, or to collect from it, how many kinds of animals there are, what are the seeds of each in their beginnings, what measure in their increase, what numbers run through their conceptions, births, ages, settings; what motions in desiring things according to their nature, and in avoiding the contrary? Have they not sought out all these things, not through that unchangeable wisdom, but through the actual history of places and times, or have trusted the written experience of others? Wherefore it is the less to be wondered at, that they have utterly failed in searching out the succession of more lengthened ages, and in finding any goal of that course, down which, as though down a river, the human race is sailing, and the transi-

---

[9]   Cf. St. Augustine's definition of history, *De doctrina christiana* II, chap. 28 no. 44; and footnote 21 in chapter three.

tion thence of each to its own proper end. For these are subjects which historians could not describe, inasmuch as they are far in the future, and have been experienced and related by no one. Nor have those philosophers, who have profited better than others in that high and eternal science, been able to grasp such subjects with the understanding; otherwise they would not be inquiring as they could into the past things of the kind, such as are in the province of the historians, but rather would foreknow also things future; and those who are able to do this are called by them soothsayers, but by us prophets.[10]

This remarkable passage clarifies the nature of philosophy of history as a branch of Christian philosophy. It will not profess to know the meaning and direction of history as a formal object of its own, cultivated by itself. It will recognize the limitation of the empirical sciences, history included: they can help to know what has existed or happened, and what is in contemporary experience. But the succession of beings and events, the *ordo temporum* with its direction and meaning, especially its future goal, lies beyond their grasp. The more it cultivates the central branch of philosophy, furthermore, "that high and eternal science" called metaphysics, the better it recognizes its inherent limitation. It can know the principles of existence which govern the being of the things which the empirical sciences study, and it can rise to Him who gives these things their participated being and its mode: but it cannot know that *ordo temporum*, the meaning, and direction of their succession in time.

Who then can? Only He who administers His creation.[11]

The philosophy of history in Christian philosophy, open to the Creator as it is, can cultivate ears to hear, in case the Supreme Being, Creator and Lord of history, has seen fit to reveal to mankind information on the plan He is developing in His creation and the contours of its origin, process, and goal. It can reflect upon the Hebrew Fact; it can experience and explain the meaning of the Catholic Fact; it can accept and study these facts as given in reality and offered to the reflection of the human thinker. But it cannot conjure up of itself, even when it

---

[10] St. Augustine, *De Trinitate* IV chap. 15 no. 20–chap. 16, no. 21; Marcus Dods, trans., *Aurelius Augustine: On the Trinity* (Edinburgh, UK: T&T Clark, 1873), 130–131; for the original text, see PL 42, 901–902.

[11] See Acts 1:6: "they asked him, 'Lord, will you at this time restore the kingdom to Israel?' He said to them, 'It is not for you to know times or seasons which the Father has fixed by his own authority.'" And again, Ecclesiastes 3.

is Metaphysics cultivated rightly, a rational insight into this meaning and direction, projecting it out from itself *as philosophy* upon the data described by the historians, and constructing thus a philosophy of history as Gnostic Modernity has thought it could do.

The first thing that Christian philosophy does is to recognize that it is not a Gnosticism in the philosophy of history. Hence, as Augustine indicates, it turns to the prophets with ears to hear, and develops its structure as a branch of philosophy by ministering to an ever better understanding of the word coming from on High through them.

THE PROPHETIC WORD

"It makes the greatest possible difference," Augustine continues, taking up the question of the prophets, "whether things future are conjectured by experience of things past ... or whether they are either foreannounced to certain men, or are heard by them and again transmitted to other men, by means of holy angels, to whom God shows these things by His Word and His Wisdom, wherein both things future and things past consist: ... [so that] the minds of certain men ... behold the immovable causes of things future in that very highest pinnacle of the universe itself."[12] These "certain men," of course, are the Hebrew prophets.

"Therefore," Augustine concludes, "neither concerning the successions of ages, nor concerning the resurrection of the dead, ought we to consult those philosophers."[13] For they build philosophies of history out of their subjective selves as mere constructs, like spiders spinning webs. It is far different in Christian philosophy, open as it is to the announcement from on High regarding the origin, meaning, and goal of history: "as these things actually were manifested to our fathers, who were gifted with true piety, and who by foretelling them, obtaining credence either by present signs, or by events close at hand, which turned out as they had foretold, earned authority to be believed respecting things remotely future, even to the end of the world."[14]

St. Augustine in his *De civitate Dei* gives the same answer to the fundamental question of the inner nature of the philosophy of history. "At present," he writes,

---

[12] Augustine, *De Trinitate* IV, chap. 17, no. 22 (Dods, 131–132).
[13] Ibid., chap. 17, no. 23 (Dods, p. 132).
[14] Ibid., (Dods, 133).

we are certain that we possess these three things [the three philosophical certitudes: that I am, that I know I am, and that I love
my known existence], not by the testimony of others but by our
own consciousness of their presence in our interior and unerr-
ing vision. Nevertheless, since we cannot know of ourselves how
long they will last or whether they will never cease and what
will result from our good or bad use of them, we seek for other
witnesses, if we have not already found them. Not now, but later,
I shall carefully discuss the reasons why we should have unhesi-
tating trust in these witnesses.[15]

Wherever human beings turn, they find themselves "among the things
which He created and has conserved so wonderfully. . . things which
belong to particular species and follow and observe their own order . . ."[16]
This is temporal creation. Science and philosophy know it validly in its
essences, in the forms, natures, and operations which it manifests. But how
long they will last; what will result from our good or bad use of them; what
the meaning of their succession is; whether it has a goal; whether it will
end, and if so, how—all this is the "philosophy of history" and it is beyond
the range of natural philosophical knowledge. The meaning of the *ordo
successionis* must be learned another way: from witnesses. What witnesses?
Men who somehow speak for the Creator, participating somehow in His
knowledge. For He alone is in a position to know the length and the direction, the origin, the meaning and the goal, of the succession of beings in
time.

It is the hallmark of Gnostic Modernity that it desired to create for
itself the order of things and hence the meaning and direction of history.
Man shall know history because he makes it himself. He will not be
content, let alone enraptured, with a meaning he finds placed there by
the Lord of history, speaking His Eternal Word. This is the taproot of
the subjective process—philosophers of the Modern Age, dreaming great
boastful "philosophies of history"—Comtean dreams, Hegelian dreams,
Marxist dreams—which deaden the mind to the voice of witnesses.

---

[15] Augustine, *De civitate Dei* XI, chap. 28 (PL 41, 341–342): "alias nunctestes vel
quaerimus vel habemus"—i.e., this kind of knowledge is in a different order, and is
not forthcoming from the natural rational power of man that produces empirical and
philosophical knowledge. For the English translation, see Gerald Walsh and Grace
Monahan, trans., *Saint Augustine: The City of God*, books VIII–XVI (Washington,
DC: Catholic University of America Press, 1963), 233.

[16] Ibid.

THE LORD OF HISTORY

The plan of the Lord of history in creating, the meaning of the temporal succession, the direction and the goal of time—all these are one; and they exist in creation because of the Word in whom God in making heaven and earth made the succession of human generations called history. In the fullness of time, this same Divine Logos was made flesh and dwelt among us. He is the chief and the greatest of the witnesses. Before Him came the witnesses called the prophets. Since His coming, mankind has the witness of the Magisterium of His Roman Catholic Church.

Thus the answer emerges to the questions regarding the nature of the philosophy of history as a branch of Christian philosophy. The ultimate causes and meaning of the temporal succession are not knowable by natural reason. Bowing its head, philosophy listens for some Word from Him who holds history in His creating power, and hence is the Lord of history.[17]

The philosophy of history in Christian philosophy, then, is basically this recognition that the *ordo temporum* is not an essence and hence cannot be known by the conventional tools of merely human empirical or philosophical knowledge. It is the secret of Him who is the Lord of history, the Creator of all its essences, substances, and natures, and the Administrator of their mutually interwoven succession in time.

Hence the first principle of philosophy of history as a branch of Christian philosophy is to cultivate an ear to hear some word from Him whom the core discipline, metaphysics, already has recognized as the intelligent Creator of the universe.

When Augustine turns to the prophets, he is not leaving the philosophy of history behind; rather, he is thinking as a philosopher of history in the most accurate and profound sense of the phrase. In doing so he is recognizing the special affinity which the philosophy of history bears to theology. This is the heart of the relationship between reason and faith, furthermore, and the specific means whereby philosophy can "supplement . . . theology in the revealing with ever increasing

---

[17] Putting these things another way, God is the master of contingency, an aspect of His almightiness which belongs strictly to the unlimited mode of existing proper to the First Cause. It belongs to God alone. The fact that there is a plan of some kind in creation and history can be deduced from the philosophical certitude that the Supreme Being of the universe is intelligent. But philosophical reason cannot know what the plan is. Voegelin puts it correctly: history is not an *eidos*, an essence.

clarity the Mystery of Christ, which affects the whole course of human history."[18]

THE CHRISTIAN PHILOSOPHY OF HISTORY

When it foregoes a positive and substantive philosophical knowledge of the *ordo temporum,* its own formal object, when it rejects the Gnosticism of the Modern Age, the Christian philosophy of history draws close to the general approach of postmodern thinking: philosophy performs a critical function rather than a substantive one.[19] But this critical function, thanks to the power of Christian metaphysics, open to the almightiness and intelligence of the Creator, and thanks to its ability to see and to reflect upon the Hebrew Fact and its Christian counterpart and fulfillment, helps to develop an understanding of the meaning and direction of history which is a unique combination of the empirically given with the light coming from the higher order of faith in the Word of God.

In the Christian philosophy of history, certain constants will be recognized in operation throughout, analogous to the constants of creation in the space-time continuum. These will be chiefly God and the human soul: *Deus Pater omnipotens, Deus totus ubique simul, Deus tam Pater,* and each soul with its time on the *machina transitura* of history decid-

---

[18] See *Optatam totius,* §14, in Austin Flannery, O.P., ed., *Vatican Council II: The Conciliar and Post Conciliar Documents* (New York: Costello, 1975), 717–718; and Josef Pieper, *Über das Ende der Zeit: Eine Geschichtsphilosophische Meditation* (Munich: Kosel-Verlag, 1953), 27: "One may say, therefore, that an affinity on principle and of a special character exists between Philosophy of History and Theology."

[19] See Henri Irénée Marrou, "Introduction: The Critical Philosophy of History," in *The Meaning of History* (Baltimore: Helicon, 1966); 9–28; R.G. Collingwood, *The Idea of History* (Oxford, UK: Clarendon Press, 1946); William Henry Walsh, *An Introduction to Philosophy of History* (London: Hutchison, 1951); Henri Gouhier, *L'histoire et sa philosophie* (Paris: J. Vrin, 1952), esp. chap. 5, "Histoire de la philosophie et histoire des visions du monde." Professor Gouhier is quite laconic: "If history has a meaning, that meaning is not historical but theological; what one calls 'philosophy of history' is never anything but a theology of history more or less disguised" (128). Better perhaps: either the objectively real one, or one of its Modernist Gnostic perversions in Voegelin's sense. For the same insight, see O. Kohler, "Geschichte," in *Lexikon fur Theologie und Kirche,* vol. 4, *Franca-Hermenegild* (Freiburg im Breisgau, DE: Herder, 1993), 777–789; "Die Sinnfrage": "Answers about meaning given by Philosophy of History are derivatives of the Theology of History" (779).

ing and choosing before the hidden face of its Maker, making itself one of His elect, or refusing to do so.[20]

Christian philosophy, furthermore, helps in the reading of the Scriptures in the literary genre in which they were written, recognizing the historicity of the historical books. For it is liberated at last from the rationalist prejudice peculiar to Modernity as such and in the new postmodern climate stands free to recognize that the Almighty, present to each moment of the space-time continuum, is at one and the same time the Creator of the universe and the Lord of history. In the light of these adequate concepts of God and Man, the Scriptural readings on the wisdom and providence of God become fully intelligible, and with them the heritage of Christian teaching on the fact and mode of divine providence both in general and in its specific character as salvation history.

---

[20] See Jacques Maritain, *On the Philosophy of History* (New York: Scribner's, 1957), 17: "The philosophy of history is connected with the whole of philosophy. And yet it itself belongs to practical and moral philosophy." Maritain did not write an *ex professo* and comprehensive treatise on the philosophy of history, but touched on it constantly when treating other questions. Cf. Charles Journet and Brooke Williams Smith, *Jacques Maritain, Antimodern or Ultramodern?—An Historical Analysis of His Critics, His Thought and His Life* (New York: Elsevier, 1976). Furthermore, his treatment tended more to concern the operation of secondary causes in history, the movement of the larger ones such as the empires, in older parlance, or cultures and civilizations, as these extensive human social entities are called today, patterns of human operation that reflect human nature. "My own reflections and remarks on the philosophy of history," he writes, "were, in fact, prompted for many years by the practical problem of the plight of Christians in contemporary society" (Maritain, 171). But Maritain gives the principles involved, and is fundamentally postmodern in his openness to the mode of the First Cause Creating as the ultimate formal object of this discipline. "The philosophy of history has the same *subject matter* as history . . . , but another *object* than history" (4). Thus he can praise Toynbee's way of characterizing the great civilizations as "a good example of the possibility of drawing through induction some typical characteristics relating to history" (9). Then his openness to the ultimate nature of the philosophy of history comes explicitly into view in his final word on Toynbee: "There is no complete or adequate philosophy of history if it is not connected with some prophetic or theological data" (170). "So it is that Toynbee's remarkable, immensely erudite and thoroughly conscientious work is finally disappointing. It misses the mark because it is too ambitious (it claims to explain history) and insufficiently equipped (it is not integrated in a general philosophy); and, above all, because it resides in a sphere entirely extraneous to moral philosophy adequately taken. Toynbee discards the possibility of having his rational inquiry assisted and complemented by a theological light and prophetic data. Hence the shallowness to which I alluded" (173). The relationship to *Optatam totius* §14 is clear. "It is in a Christian perspective," Maritain states, "that I have for a long time brooded over my reflections on the philosophy of history" (54).

7

MODERNITY AS
APOSTASY FROM GOD

I T is this philosophy of history, then, with ears to hear rather than eyes to see, which the renewal of Christian philosophy carries with it into the postmodern situation of reality and of thought. Can it possibly still be valid? Can it have survived its centuries-long intellectual denigration at the hands of proud Modernity? Or is it not itself simply another construct like that which prevailed from Petrarch to Voltaire, which came into bloom in those grandiose nineteenth century philosophies of history of Comte, Hegel, and Karl Marx?

In answer, the Christian thinker has something new he can do which was impossible for Augustine. He can continue to point with Augustine to the Hebrew Fact and the Catholic Fact as an empirical base in history itself for his philosophizing and theologizing about meaning and direction and goal.

But now he can also observe a new fact, likewise a given in history. It is the qualitative character of Modern philosophy, as such and as a whole, studied as the fountainhead of the secularization of Western education and culture.

That Modern philosophy is a philosophical essence, a particular kind of philosophizing located in space and time, has been noted above. Modern philosophy has a preparation in Petrarch and the Renaissance, a birth in Descartes and Spinoza, a ripened fulfillment in Kant, Comte, Hegel, and Marx, and an ending in the carnage of World War I and the consequent disillusionment, when philosophy becomes self-aware as postmodern.

THE HISTORICITY OF MODERN PHILOSOPHY

Now is the time, postmodern time, to inquire into the existential dynamism of Modern philosophy. Does this philosophical essence fit in any meaningful way into the panorama of historical succession? Does Modern philosophy itself, as such, have meaning precisely in this dimension? This is to ask the question which constitutes the philosophy of history as a branch of philosophy; and it is Christian philosophy alone which stands erect in the rubble of the twentieth century, able to ask the question and to indicate the place where the answer may be heard.

Can this philosophical essence of Modern philosophy be isolated by analysis and identified by research? It can indeed, and the scholars exist who have pioneered the way.[1] This essence is constituted by two fundamental notes. The first is a falling away from the transcendent personal God of creation and revelation. Lip service to "God" as a pantheistic deception or as a mere abstraction of the human mind frequently remains. But the living God is no longer present. Mathematics replaces metaphysics and the first six arts plunge into an unbridled type of dedication to this cosmos and turn in upon man in a new way. The second note results immediately. It is the production of men of sin who refuse the very idea of abiding and objective moral principles coming from the divine Being and His Eternal Law.

Seen thus from the postmodern position and evaluated by the principles of the postmodern metaphysics, open once again to the personal God of creation, Modern philosophy stands qualitatively quite finished in the mind's eye and becomes intelligible as itself a fulfillment of the Scriptures, as a given in history comparable to the Hebrew Fact and the Catholic Fact.[2]

This distinctive quality, unheard of in all the earlier history of human thought and culture, is the atheistic character of Modern philosophy as such, and the consequent aversion of the Voltairean philosophy of

---

[1]   Cf. the works of Cornelio Fabro and Georg Siegmund in note 7 in chapter four, abiding postmodern foundations for further study of the matter; and the four-volume work of Giulio Girardi, ed., *L'ateismo contemporaneo* (Torino, IT: Societa Editrice Internazionale, 1967–1970), helpful for its accumulation of facts and references. For his brief statement of his conclusion, that the principle of immanence is virtual atheism, see Cornelio Fabro, "Filosofia moderna e ateismo," *Humanitas* (1961): 481–492.

[2]   See 2 Thess 2:1–12, esp. 3–4: "The Day of the Lord . . . cannot happen until the Great Revolt has taken place . . ." (Jerusalem Bible).

history from the Hebrew and Catholic Facts. These characteristics give Modernity its peculiar color and tone which the Christian philosopher can only evaluate as a great apostasy from God, a great revolt against God the Creator, God the Redeemer, and God the Sanctifier of mankind.[3]

FRIEDRICH NIETZSCHE

There are two central figures in the philosophical research which brings Modernity into view as a great revolt against God, and very possibly as the Great Apostasy, genius-types who experienced this fact to the full and analyzed it with profound insight. One is Friedrich Nietzsche, who is helpful from a negative point of view: for his *Entwertung aller Werte*, his emptying of content from all human values, which was the meaning of his proclamation of the Death of God, refers precisely to Modernity as a loss of the *intelligibilia*, the intellectual principles for thought and for life that follow from philosophical recognition of the Supreme Being. Nothing remains but the reduction of the human mode of existing to what Heidegger will term *Dasein,* the organismic and animal experience of existence confined to, imprisoned within, this world. This can be cast into various temporary Superman roles, but the reality always surfaces: *Nothing* remains. Nietzsche himself knew it in the nineteenth century and saw Nihilism coming as a widespread social condition in the century to follow his own.[4]

---

3   See Arnold Toynbee, *A Study of History* (London: Oxford University Press, 1934–1954), 6:535: "What is at stake in this debate is nothing else than the essence of the Christian Faith: the threefold belief in the love of God, in His Incarnation in Jesus Christ, and in His perpetual operation in this World through the Holy Spirit." Toynbee points accurately here to the Profession of the Apostolic Faith, the Apostles' Creed, which constitutes the baptismal apostolicity of the Church and which has built the Catholic Fact into what Augustine called the Sixth Age, and what we call the Christian Era.

4   For Nietzsche's "Death of God" theme, see the episode of "Der tolle Mench" in *Die fröhliche Wissenschaft,* in *Werke,* vol. 2 (Munich: Karl Hanser Verlag, 1955), 126ff.: "*Wir haben ihn getötet*—ihr und ich! Wir alle sind seine Mörder. Aber wie haben wir dies gemacht?" (127). "But how have we done this?" This is indeed the ultimate question which Modernity must ask itself. Heidegger, Nietzsche's foremost disciple, gives the answer in "Nietzsche's Wort, 'Gott ist tot,'" in *Holzwege* (Frankfurt, DE: Klostermann, 1963), 193–247. It was done, Heidegger says accurately, by subverting the historic Christian *paideia,* the Christian education of youth which sustained the edifice of Christian culture. The subversion was a philosophical one, the introduction of Modern philosophy with its characteristic inability to see the *intelligibilia,* the abiding truths of the intelligence, because it had eliminated metaphysics and substituted mathematical physics for it. Thus young people were denied a solid foundation

JOHN HENRY NEWMAN

John Henry Newman is the other figure, positive where the unhappy Nietzsche is purely negative. For Newman's thought provides a positive analysis of Modernity from the viewpoint of education which in turn gives the Christian philosophy of history its new empirical base. This is fundamentally important, for it saves this philosophy of history from lapsing into one more mere subjective construct. "It is this Christian philosophy of history," writes Christopher Dawson, "that underlies the whole of Newman's doctrine on education."[5] For Newman knew well that the edifice of Christian culture, and indeed, humanly speaking, the Church herself, cannot stand unless the Christianized *paideia* of *Roma Christiana* is maintained intact. This is doubly true when it is a question of educating young men for the priesthood and of training catechists for the Ministry of the Word. The corrosive action of Modern philosophy, when it filters into the other six arts and governs the raising of children and the preparation of the personnel who lead and guide civic and social life, results in permissiveness and superficiality.

"They leave their place of education," Newman writes with prophetic insight, "simply dissipated and relaxed by the multiplicity of subjects, which they have never really mastered, and so shallow as not even to know their own shallowness."[6] Such a person "... can utter a number of truths or sophisms, as the case may be, and one is as good to him as another. He is up with a number of doctrines and a number of facts, but they are all loose and straggling, for he has no principles set up in his mind round which to aggregate and locate them" but only "a barren mockery of knowledge"; "he sees objections more clearly than truths, and can ask a thousand questions which the wisest of men cannot answer; and withal, he has a very good opinion of himself, and is well satisfied with his attainments."[7]

---

for the values, whether natural or Christian. The "Death of God" is the eclipse of the *intelligibilia* in the education of youth. The answer to Nietzsche's question, "Aber wie haben wir dies gemacht?" ("But how have we done this?") lies in the field of philosophy linked with education: in the philosophy of education. John Henry Newman agrees completely: this is the very idea of his *Idea of a University* (London: Longmans, Green, and Co., 1947).

[5]   Christopher Dawson, "Education and the Study of Christian Culture," *Studies* (Autumn, 1953): 297, citing the whole of Newman's Lecture, "Christianity and Letters," in *The Idea of a University*.

[6]   Newman, *The Idea of a University*, 132.

[7]   Ibid., 371. When vigilant care is not exercised in the education and training of priests and catechists, what Newman saw and foresaw can become visible inside the Church.

Seen thus from the field of education and its gradual de-Christianization and subversion, Modernity looks quite different to the postmodern thinker than it did in the Modern Age. It is no longer a promise of all truth and social welfare; it appears rather as an apostasy which took on a social form, to dominate ever more completely over Christian education and culture. In the twentieth century, the experience of this falling away from God is manifold, an experience which, in their keen way of genius, thinkers like Juan Donoso Cortes and John Henry Newman anticipated a hundred years ago.

"I believe that the Catholic civilization contains the good without admixture of evil," Donoso Cortes cried out in the Parliament at Madrid at mid-nineteenth century, "and that the philosophical civilization contains the evil without admixture of good. . . . By representing the Empire of Faith as dead, and by proclaiming the independence of human reason and will, it has rendered absolute, universal and necessary the evil which before was relative, exceptional and contingent."[8]

Newman likewise perceived and described Modernity as a process moving from a Christian condition of personal thought and social life toward an anti-Christian one. "I grant," he writes, "that as Rome, according to the prophet Daniel's vision, succeeded Greece, so Antichrist succeeds Rome, and the Second Coming succeeds Antichrist. But it does not hence follow that Antichrist is come: for it is not clear that the Roman Empire is gone."[9] Newman was keenly conscious, however, of witnessing and experiencing some special kind of revolt against God. Over a half century before the postmodern breakthrough, he had his finger on the nature of Modernity: "Surely, there is at this day a confederacy of evil, marshalling its hosts from all parts of the world, organizing itself, taking its measures, enclosing the Church of Christ as in a net, and preparing the way for a general Apostasy from it."[10]

From the viewpoint of its social and pedagogical background, Newman is indispensable for understanding the phenomenon of Religious Modernism. One might perhaps say that Newman projects accurately the "mind" of certain segments of the 20th century episcopate and priesthood. See, for example, 370–373, and 296: "It is a miserable time when a man's Catholic profession is no voucher for his orthodoxy, and when a teacher of Religion may be within the Church's pale, yet external to her Faith."

[8] Juan Donoso Cortes, quoted in Denis de Rougemont, *The Idea of Europe* (London: Collier-Macmillan, 1966), 267.

[9] John Henry Newman, *Discussions and Arguments on Various Subjects* (London: Longman's, 1899), 50.

[10] Ibid., 60.

THE SUBVERSION OF EDUCATION

Paradoxically, it is the very victory of Modernity over the Catholic Fact in society which has opened the way to the postmodern intellectual victory for the Christian philosophy of history, precisely because the Faith itself ever since the Apostles has expected an Apostasy from God and the advent of a new empire following upon that of Christian Rome.

For it is now a commonplace that the Christianized *paideia* which sustained Western civilization across its Christian centuries has become increasingly subverted since Rousseau's *Emile,* the philosophy of education written at the time and in the context of the Voltairean philosophy of history.[11] For not only has the Christian mode in education and culture been increasingly eliminated, but the very substance of the *paideia* in itself, as something natural to man is being lost. The millennial concept of a disciplined training and perfecting of the naturally given is disappearing. Without the adjective Christian, Modernity has made it clear that the *paideia* itself cannot survive. *Wachsen lassen,* mere natural growth, mere nature as already perfect and having but to unfold: these are the concepts which have come to dominate childrearing and the education of youth.[12]

For those who philosophized in the older mode of Modern philosophy, from a position separated from the Faith, this seemed to promise a new age of progress and liberation. But for those whose philosophy of history is linked with a metaphysics open to God and the Soul and is built upon a theocentric *paideia* as St. Augustine grounds it in book one of his *De doctrina christiana,* the dissolution of the historic Christian *paideia* will appear to be nothing else than a great social apostasy from God. For without the enculturation of youth into the Christian culture

---

[11] In 1762 Rousseau published his *Emile, or, Concerning Education;* approximately one eighth of the text, customarily omitted in English versions, is devoted to "The Confession of the Savoyard Vicar," Rousseau's explanation of his own naturalistic religiosity. He uses this clergyman whom he conjures up, often called the first Modernist priest, to do the explaining.

[12] See note 4, above, on Heidegger's pedagogical interpretation of Nietzsche's dictum, the Death of God. For further research on this matter, one must analyze Rousseau's *Emile* as the background for John Dewey's *The Influence of Darwin on Philosophy* (in *The Influence of Darwin on Philosophy and Other Essays* [New York: Henry Holt and Company, 1910]) and *Democracy and Education: An Introduction to the Philosophy of Education* (New York: MacMillan, 1922); works which fasten the Death of God—the revolt against God—upon America, and move it toward the whole world as "The American Way of Life."

of *Roma conversa,* the Roman Empire in its Christianized form cannot stand. In the parlance of contemporary students of comparative culture, the foundations of Western Civilization will have been eroded away.

Thus, for those with eyes to see the empirically given, together with ears to hear the Prophetic Word, the Christian philosophy of history, born in Augustine's *De civitate Dei* and *De doctrina christiana,* has a contemporary timeliness. It is quite at home, once again, in the postmodern situation. For it gives the Christian thinker an insight into the fact and the cause of an utterly new social situation of mankind, that of the ripening of the conditions for a new *translatio imperii,* a new "transfer of Empire," to him perhaps whom Christian tradition knows as the Man of Sin, and expects in connection with a Great Apostasy from God.[13]

---

[13] For the seminal treatment of this mysterious matter in Christian thought, see Augustine's *De civitate Dei* bk. 20, chap. 8–30. The delay in the *parousia,* that article in the Profession of the Apostolic Faith linked intrinsically with the redeeming death and the resurrection of Jesus the Messiah, has been a problem for members of the Church from the beginning, since 2 Thess 2:1–12. Perhaps the philosophy of history is now in a position to cooperate with theology in understanding the matter better. For it was an unhappy effect of Modern philosophy as such, as Leo XIII stated in *Aeterni Patris,* to undermine the liberal disciplines in their Christianized form which functioned as the dynamic social foundation of *Roma Christiana,* the historic edifice of Christian culture. Newman's greatness lies in his masterful analysis of this negative phenomenon from the viewpoint of the philosophy of education. For he saw that this phenomenon evokes permissivist "men of sin" who are not formed to know and to value the Way of Life, which consists of definite moral positions and principles. Thus Newman's analysis of the situation in modern Western education becomes the philosophical tool for recognizing the apostasy as something empirically given and knowable by the light of sound natural reason. Newman grasps the philosophical and social principles which make intelligible that immensely grand succession in human history which he himself states in lapidary form in the passage cited in the text above: "I grant, that as Rome, according to the prophet Daniel's vision, succeeded Greece, so Antichrist succeeds Rome, and the Second Coming succeeds Antichrist" (*Discussions and Arguments,* 50). The experience of Modernity and the perception of it as apostasy from God is clear in the documents of the Holy See since about 1740 when the encyclical letter was adopted by Rome as the ordinary vehicle of its apostolate to the modern world. This is especially true from Pope Pius IX to the present. This entire matter calls for a separate study; it might well bear significant fruit for both the philosophy and the theology of history. Furthermore, such a study could reveal in a new way the prophetic role of the Holy See standing among the increasingly apostate Gentile nations of the Modern period of the Christian Era.

8

INTELLECTUAL VICTORY
OVER MODERNISM

THE phenomenon of Modernism in religion may seem at first sight irrelevant in a discussion of the philosophy of history. Exactly the opposite is true, however, for Religious Modernism is the product and function of the philosophy of history in its older Voltairean and Hegelian form.

Hence it is impossible to do comprehensive research in this branch of philosophy without taking it into consideration.[1] This kind of analysis, furthermore, has great practical value for priestly and catechetical teaching, for the philosophy of history is the best instrument for unmasking the nature of Modernism, for parrying its deception, and for winning a true victory over it for the cause of authentic religious thinking.[2]

---

[1] So large a subject can be sketched only briefly here, in the hope of stimulating further discussion and research on the part of younger Catholic scholars, minds increasingly free of the inhibitions and philosophical inadequacies holding over into the twentieth century from the Modern period.

[2] See the *General Catechetical Directory* (Washington, DC: USCC, 1971), no. 88: "Catechesis . . . simply cannot neglect the formation of a religious way of thinking. . . . It must provide the natural foundations for faith with the greatest care." This can be done today only by coming to grips with the phenomenon of Religious Modernism, unmasking its nature and exposing its philosophically outdated character. In no. 849 of his postmodern spiritual classic *The Way* (New York: Image/Doubleday, 2006), St. Josemaria Escriva writes: "Come on! Ridicule him! Tell him he is behind the times: it is incredible that there are still people who insist on regarding the stagecoach as a good

THE GENESIS OF MODERNISM

Modernism in religion is a phenomenon of the "Modern" period of Western Civilization, the specific result of an application of Modern philosophy to the Judeo-Christian religious tradition. Cornelio Fabro describes its genesis accurately: it is "that penetration of Modern Philosophy into the seminaries which produces the phenomenon which comes soon to receive the name of Modernism."[3]

This insight, furthermore, applies equally well to all three branches of the Western religious heritage. When Modern philosophy, as such, was introduced into the training of young men as Rabbis, Reform Judaism resulted and is sustained. When the same was done in training for the Protestant Ministry, Liberal Protestantism resulted and is sustained. In all three cases, the general effect is an undermining of faith in the historicity of the sources of each religious tradition, a reinterpretation of these sources in such a way that a new kind of religion begins to function within their organizational frameworks and didactic terminologies. They are thus gradually transformed into what Karl Jaspers aptly terms philosophical faith directed more at the cultivation of immanent human powers on the natural level than religious faith directed toward an order of revealed truth and knowledge, distinct in origin and in object, coming from the personal God standing transcendent above nature.[4]

---

means of transportation. That is for those who dig up musty, old-fashioned 'Voltairianisms' or discredited liberal ideas of the nineteenth century."

[3] Cornelio Fabro, *Breve introduzione al Tomismo* (Rome: Desclee, 1960), 73. In this connection, cf. the special issue of *Divinitas* (1958): 3–190, in commemoration of the fiftieth anniversary of the Encyclical *Pascendi,* a mine of information valuable both in itself and in the light of the two ensuing decades. This issue presents a number of studies by experts on the Modernist problem especially in the matter of preparing young men for the priesthood; see, in particular, Roberto Masi, "L'insegnamento dell'Enciclica *Pascendi* contra gli errori dei Modernisti sulla conoscenza di Dio," (51–68); and Luigi Ciappi, O.P., "La Persona di Gesù Cristo nell' Enciclica *Pascendi,*" (69–84).

[4] Thus it is true to say that Spinoza is the metaphysician of modern atheism, and to recognize the direct line of paternity that reaches from him to unsound Scripture scholarship. See Emile Poulat, *Une oeuvre clandestine d'Henry Bremond* (Rome: Edizioni di Storia e Letteratura, 1972), 117–118: "Richard Simon (1638–1712) during the Modernist crisis was one of the symbols of the conflict in which men were engaged: Loisy and his friends saw Richard Simon as their precursor, while Batiffol denounced his approach." For the concept "philosophical faith" see Karl Jaspers, *Philosophical Faith and Revelation* (New York: Harper and Row, 1967); and St. Thomas Aquinas, *Summa Theologica* II–II, q. 5, a. 3:

EFFECT OF THE MAGISTERIUM

While this phenomenon is powerfully present in Protestantism and Judaism, its impact within the Catholic Church in the formal and technical sense of "Modernism" is altogether unique. The reason for this bears much further research; but the cause appears to be the presence and the actions of the Magisterium, that teaching authority which is unique in Catholicity.

To bring this into better visibility, the Hebrew Fact and its fulfillment as the Catholic Fact in history must be reviewed. It is interesting to note the insight of the Protestant scholar Kirsopp Lake in his introduction to Eusebius' *Ecclesiastical History*.

"The object of the whole book," he writes,

> was to present the Christian "Succession," which did not merely mean, though it certainly included, the apostolic succession of the bishops of the four great "thrones," but rather the whole intellectual, spiritual and institutional life of the Church. It cannot be too strongly emphasized that Eusebius, like all early church historians, can be understood only if it be recognized that whereas modern writers try to trace the development, growth, and change of doctrines and institutions, their predecessors were trying to prove that nothing of the kind ever happened. According to them the Church had had one and only one teaching from the beginning; it had been preserved by the "Succession" and heresy was the attempt of the Devil to change it.[5]

The Catholic Fact, in other words, is constituted dynamically in history by evangelization and catechesis: by a doctrinal teaching, that is, which centers upon the Articles of Faith in Jesus Christ as the Apostolic *kerygma* or Creed professes Him to be. This is the "Ordinary and Uni-

---

It is manifest that he who adheres to the teaching of the Church, as to an infallible rule, assents to whatever the Church teaches; otherwise, if, on the things taught by the Church, he holds what he chooses to hold and rejects what he chooses to reject, he no longer adheres to the teaching of the Church as to an infallible rule, but to his own will. . . . Therefore it is clear that such a heretic with regard to one article has no faith in the other articles, but only a kind of opinion in accordance with his own will.

5 Kirsopp Lake, trans., *Eusebius: The Ecclesiastical History* (Cambridge: Harvard University Press, 1953), 1:xxxiv–xxxv.

versal Magisterium" which was the object of formal definition by the First Vatican Council.[6] This teaching program maintains the Catholic Fact in social reality as the generations of members of the Church move forward in time.

From the beginning, Catholic thinkers have recognized in this living Magisterium the proximate Rule of Faith. The early Church Fathers elaborated this point in detail against a kaleidoscope of Gnostic doctrinal innovations in the Argument from Prescription.[7] Vincent of Lerins gave it its classical statement which the Magisterium has made its own in every century since, and especially in Vatican I, Vatican II, and the documents of Popes John XXIII and Paul VI.[8]

---

[6]   Pius IX, Dogmatic Constitution *Dei Filius*, April 24, 1870, chap. 3: "All those matters must be believed with divine and Catholic faith that are contained in the word of God, whether in Scripture or tradition, and that are proposed by the Church, either by a solemn decision or by the ordinary and universal magisterium, to be believed as divinely revealed" (John Broderick, S.J. trans., *Documents of Vatican I* [Collegeville, MD: The Liturgical Press, 1971], 44). For the fact that "all those matters" are summarized in the Creed and the official catechisms by which the bishops explain its Articles of Faith, see J.M.A. Vacant, "De la foi," in *Etudes théologiques sur les Constitutions du Concile du Vatican* (Paris: Delhomme et Briguet, 1895), 2:15–179, and esp. 89–95, "Qu'est ce que le magistère ordinaire et universel de l'Eglise?"

[7]   For the proximate Rule of Faith, see Emmanuel Doronzo, *The Channels of Revelation* (Middleburg, VA: Notre Dame Institute Press, 1974), esp. chapter 3, "The Magisterium, Organ of Revelation," 33–37 and chapter 4, "Dogma," 39–51, with the literature; and Charles Journet, *Le dogme chemin de la foi* (Paris: Fayard, 1963) with the valuable discussion of bibliography on the point, 103–104, omitted in the English translation, *What is Dogma?* (New York: Hawthorn, 1965). Also E. Kevane, *Creed and Catechetics* (Westminster, MD: Christian Classics, 1978), a presentation of the Creed of the People of God as the contemporary "Rule of Faith" for teachers of the Catholic Faith; see, in particular, the discussion of the literature on the point, 260–263.

[8]   See Vincent of Lerins, *Commonitorium* (PL 50, 688): "sed in suo dumtaxat genere, in eodem scilicet dogmate, eodem sensu eademque sententia." This phrase, referring to the fundamental fact which preserves the Apostolicity of the Catholic Church as an historical fact and reality across the centuries, was cited by Vatican I (Denziger and Schönmetzer, ed., *Enchiridion*, no. 3020 [hereafter DS]), by Pope John XXIII in his discourse which opened Vatican II (cf. AAS 54 [1962], 785), by Vatican II itself (cf. *Gaudium et spes*, no. 62; AAS 58 [1966], 1083), and by Pope Paul VI in his actions to meet the "Crisis of Faith" that began to emerge into public view almost immediately after Vatican II (cf. Apostolic Exhortation announcing the Year of Faith *Petrum et Paulum Apostolos* [Feb 22, 1967] in AAS 59 [1967], pp. 193–200; and his Allocution opening the Synod of Bishops, ibid., 963–969). The significance of this ongoing presence of the Catholic Fact in postmodern times is of course fundamental for a contemporary philosophy of history.

ELIMINATION OF THE ENTIRE CREED

It is this "prescription," as the Early Church termed it, this "Ordinary and Universal Magisterium" in the words of Vatican I, which Modernism sets aside. Unlike earlier heretical movements, it takes its position not against this or that particular Article of Faith, but against the Profession of the Apostolic Faith as such.[9] This is done by a reinterpretation, as it is called, of the entire Creed in the light of Modern philosophy. A writer in the Encyclopedia Britannica puts it accurately: the Modernists "sought to reinterpret traditional Catholic teaching in the light of 19th-century philosophical, historical, and psychological theories."[10] Participating in the essential characteristics of Modern philosophy as such, in its Cartesian, Spinozan, and Kantian metaphysics, it introduces into religious thought the eclipse of the transcendent personal God of Revelation characteristic of Modern philosophy, and hence its shift toward man-centrism, toward positivism, and empiricism in epistemology. Faith, the very heart of religion, is the first element to suffer this reinterpretation: it is now an experience of the Divine (as the God of Abraham comes to be called) and not an intellectual assent to the Word of God revealed and committed to a teaching Church to hand on by means of the human discourse of evangelization and catechesis.[11] Once

---

[9] See Charles Journet, *The Church of the Word Incarnate* (London: Sheed and Ward, 1955), 1:543:

> It is not to be believed, say the Modernists, that God has revealed through Christ and the Apostles any definitive truth to be received by the intelligence and preserved intact forever. All that God did—insofar as it is possible to speak about God at all—was to move the souls of the Apostles, and these then attempted to translate their experience into more or less happy conceptual formulas, not in the least to be taken for a "divine law" or as binding on later generations. A genuine apostolicity therefore does not consist of the handing down of an unaltered doctrine; it consists in a reliving by each of us of that experience of divine things which Christ and the Apostles lived so admirably, and in translating it perhaps for ourselves into a new conceptual synthesis better adapted to a changing world. The mark of apostolicity will be rather innovation than tradition, doctrinal fluidity rather than the immobility of the *Credo*.

If Religious Modernism were to have its way, in other words, changing evangelization and catechetics as it proposes to do, the Catholic Fact would disappear from view on earth and in history. As Journet points out, apostolicity is the constitutive mark of the Church.

[10] *Encyclopedia Britannica*, Vol. XV, p. 631.

[11] The Magisterium of the Catholic Church has been concerned with this problem consistently throughout all three moments of Religious Modernism. The best-known

this subversion of the eternal concept of truth has taken place in the realm of Faith, all the rest follows, and the reinterpretation of the Creed as a whole begins the logic of its course.

It is quite apparent, therefore, that an immense summational heresy is at work, and that the phenomenon is far larger than this or that incident in connection with one decade or another of the Modern period in Western history.

The philosopher of history will see it more comprehensively in connection with Modernity as such and as a whole, and indeed in terms of the precise analysis of Modernity accomplished increasingly by post-modern thinkers.[12] The task which remains here, then, is to locate this

---

document is of course Pius X's Encyclical Letter on the Doctrines of the Modernists *Pascendi* (Sep 8, 1907) but it is only one among many. In the decades prior to Vatican I, there are the letters of the Holy See to the bishops of Germany regarding the spread of the doctrine of Relativism among priests teaching in the universities and seminaries. Pope Leo XIII was involved with the second moment throughout his pontificate; in this respect the work of Pius X is only a continuation and completion of his own. And it is becoming clear that Vatican II took place in the context of the emerging third moment, and that the pontificate of Pope Paul VI was dealing with it day in and day out, under the heading of the "Crisis of Faith." See his documents connected with the Year of Faith, culminating with the Solemn Profession of Faith known as the *Creed of the People of God,* his remarkable allocution of January 19, 1972 in which he cites explicitly the chief documents of Pius X, and indeed his pontificate as a whole. See *L'Osservatore Romano* English Edition (Jan 27, 1972), 1, 12; reprinted in E. Kevane, *Creed and Catechetics,* 205–208.

[12] For example, in the works of Eric Voegelin, cited above. Cf. the summary judgment of Pius X in *Pascendi,* no. 39: "And now with our eyes fixed upon the whole system . . . of the Modernists, no one will be surprised that we should define it to be the synthesis of all heresies"; cf. Vincent A. Yzermans, ed., *All Things in Christ: Encyclicals and Selected Documents of St. Pius X* (Westminster, MD: The Newman Press, 1954), 117. The refusal to see the Modernist phenomenon comprehensively contains more than might at first sight meet the eye. It is actually a deceptive intellectual tactic which the centenary of *Aeterni Patris* ought to consider carefully. The tactic begins by consigning to oblivion the first or German phase of the phenomenon, the actual occasion for Vatican I without which that Council is not properly intelligible. It then takes up its consideration of the phenomenon with Loisy and Tyrrell, the leaders of the second phase, praising them for "identifying the problem" correctly, but faulting them for their early clumsiness and pioneering inexpertness in solving it. And the tactic proceeds victoriously in what is called the "spirit" of Vatican II, proclaiming that only "now" can the problem-solving hermeneutical principles be put into operation which at last resolve the entire matter successfully. Certain recent Catholic encyclopedias omit "Günther" entirely. For a full-dress presentation of the tactic, see Roger Aubert, "Die modernistische Krise" in H. Jedin, ed., *Die Kirche der Gegenwart, Zweiter Halbband: Die Kirche zwischen Anpassung und Widerstand (1878 bis 1914)* (Freiburg, DE: Herder, 1973), 435–500. "The crisis which concerns us here," Aubert writes, "runs on a line in a certain sense parallel

religious phenomenon more accurately in the Modern Age and to bring it into view first as a function of Modern philosophy as such and then as an application of its philosophy of history, the sequence of the three constructs, "Ancient," "Medieval," and "Modern."

It is of fundamental importance to recognize that Modernism in the Catholic Church has not had that simple and unimpeded development which has characterized the growth of Reform Judaism and Liberal Protestantism. Catholic Modernism, beginning indeed at the same time and from the same causes, was interrupted in such a way by actions of the Magisterium that it exists historically in three separate moments of time.

THE THREE PHASES OF MODERNISM

The first moment, the decades of the nineteenth century prior to the First Vatican Council, is identified by the work of a group of priests, chiefly German, under the leadership of Father Anton Günther (1783–1863). Enamored with the Modern philosophy of Descartes and Kant, alienated from the patrimony of Christian philosophy, Güntherism taught that the dogmas of faith are infallibly true, indeed, but only with a relative truth: relative to the progress reached by science and philosophy at the time of the dogmatic definition. As this progress advances, the articles and dogmas of faith must be reinterpreted accordingly. Definitions and formulations of faith, the best possible when the Church first stated them, become outmoded with the passage of time, and, quite simply, must be replaced. Thus the dogmas develop intrinsically, just as

---

to the crisis which surfaced a half-century earlier in the Churches of the Reformation under the name of a 'Liberal Protestantism'" (436). This is indeed a smooth consignment to oblivion of the Catholic priest-professors in German universities who were part of the immediate occasion for the calling of Vatican I. Aubert exemplifies the other aspects of the tactic as well: cf. his treatment of "Pius X: ein konservativen Reformpapst" (ibid., 391–405), which seems predicated upon a false criterion for identifying "the problems" and upon an unsound philosophical base for solving them. It was exactly the role of Vatican I and of *Aeterni Patris* to provide the intellectual foundations needed in this matter. One may be permitted to observe that this illustrates a surprising lack of comprehensiveness and objectivity in empirical scholarship, together with an equally surprising shallowness in philosophical analysis. It does *Aeterni Patris* in, so to speak, and worse still it ends by pitting Vatican II against Vatican I, dividing the mind of Christ in His Body which is the Church. It is actually a myopic view which makes it impossible either to see the significance of *Aeterni Patris* during its first century, or to celebrate its centenary, or to perceive its abiding relevance in the coming times of its second century.

science and philosophy do. There is no absolute truth in the Catholic
Fact, but only a relative truth, always more perfectible.

This is so because the idea of Revelation itself is changed: the object
of Revelation is not a *locutio Dei,* a Word of God communicated in
human discourse by a Church sent to teach. The problem is in the First
Article of the Creed, obscured by the characteristic influence of Modern
philosophy, casting a shadow of eclipse over the transcendent personal
God of creation. Thus Giordano Bruno was correct when he selected
as his motto, *veritas filia temporis*—truth is the daughter of time. Faith
is rooted in religious experience rather than in the evangelization and
catechetics of the teaching Church. And the Hegelian dialectic with its
historicism, its outmoding of the past, is accepted as the norm of Christian thinking.[13]

The second moment emerges after Vatican I, from the Encyclical of
Leo XIII, *Providentissimus Deus* (1898), to the firm actions of Pope St.
Pius X in 1908, when Fathers Loisy and Tyrrell were excommunicated.
They stood at the head of a current of priestly thought located this time
primarily in France, Italy, and England. From the philosophical point of
view, it represents simply an adaptation of Güntherism, and its translation into the other languages which are concerned.

The third moment surfaced shortly after Vatican II, and was identified officially by Pope Paul VI in *Petrum et Paulum Apostolos* (Feb 22,
1967), the document which announced the Year of Faith and explained
the reason for it: the doctrinal aberrations that result from the contin-

---

[13] See Pius IX, *Dei Filius* as a whole, and in particular chap. 4 with its canons (DS,
nos. 3015–3020, 3041–3043). Güntherism was the immediate occasion which led
Pope Pius IX to call for the First Vatican Council. For the study of the philosophical identity of the three moments, see L. Billot, *De immutabilitate Traditionis contra
modernam haeresim evolutionismi,* 4th ed. (Rome: Gregorian University Press, 1929).
Leads for the study of this first or German moment of the Modernist phenomenon
can be found in DS, nos. 2738–2740, 2828–2831, 2850–2861, 2875–2880, and in
general 2890–2980. And cf. Ladislas Orban, *Theologia Guntheriana et Concilium
Vaticanum,* vols. 1–2 (Rome: Gregorian University Press, 1950). It is surprising to
note the same oblivion of this first phase (mentioned in note 12 above) in Oskar
Schroeder, *Aufbruch und Missverständnis: Zur Geschichte der Reformkatholischen
Bewegung* (Graz, AU: Verlag Styria, 1969): after an opening chapter on Lamennais,
Schroeder leaps many decades forward to the second moment, to chapters on Loisy,
Tyrrell, Buonaiuti, Von Hugel, and the rest. His chapter on *Reformkatholizismus* in
Germany begins with Herman Schell (1850–1906), definitely a figure of the second
moment. Neither Vatican I nor *Aeterni Patris* appear in the book. The same total
oblivion of the first or German phase characterizes the work of Claude Tresmontant,
La Crise Moderniste (Paris: Seuil, 1979).

uing advocacy of the characteristic philosophical positions of the older Modern period. Again from the viewpoint of philosophical analysis, this third moment represents nothing new, and is best understood as an organized popularization of Güntherism and the "Modernism" of the opening years of the present century.[14]

VICTORY OVER MODERNISM

In the light of the foregoing considerations, the intellectual victory over Modernism is not difficult to accomplish, whether in personal thought or in ecclesiastical teaching. For this victory does indeed have these two

---

[14] The superficial observer, standing in the flotsam and jetsam of the flooding third moment, can miss the fact that Religious Modernism in the Catholic Church is one unified intellectual phenomenon, philosophically identical throughout its history and in each of its three moments of special historical visibility. See Billot, *De immutabilitate Traditionis.* At the core of this unity, as the Holy See has recognized over and over, is philosophical relativism, the concept of truth characteristic of Modern philosophy as such. This is why the renewal of Christian philosophy is so timely and such an abiding pastoral necessity. Much research remains to be done on this underlying unity. A comparative study, for example, of Anton Günther at mid-nineteenth century and of his contemporary popularizers is a need of the day. As samples, and to draw attention to the kind of material available for such a comparative analysis, a North American might mention Avery Dulles' *Survival of Dogma,* the writings of certain of his associates at the Catholic University of America in Washington, the editorial statements and orientation of *Theological Studies,* now at the same University, and the like. A second area where research is waiting to be done is the philosophical preparations for the third moment of the phenomenon. The beginnings appear in Armand Colin, ed., *Bulletin de la Société Francaise de Philosophie* (March 21, 1931): the record of the defense of the very idea of Christian philosophy by Maritain and Gilson, against the attack upon it led by the atheistic thinkers Brunschvicg and Bréhier; and in the record of the famous Juvisy Conference of the Société Thomiste (September 11–12, 1932), published as *La philosophie chretienne* (Paris: Cerf, 1933), where, to Gilson's surprise, a group of priest-philosophers rose to defend the position of Brunschvicq and Brehier. Gilson recognized immediately that this intellectual disobedience opens a fissure in the program for the renewal of Christian philosophy in the institutions of Catholic Higher Education. Gilson's analysis of the episode is to be found in his *Christianity and Philosophy* (New York: Sheed and Ward, 1939), 82–102. Pope Paul VI recognized many times the holdover character of the philosophical substrate for the third moment of the phenomenon. See his document calling for the Year of Faith, *Petrum et Paulum Apostolos,* February 22, 1967 (AAS 59 [1967], 193–200); for the English see E. Kevane, *Creed and Catechetics,* 164–170. The Pope speaks of "New opinions in exegesis and theology often borrowed from bold but blind secular philosophies (which) have in places found a way into the realm of Catholic teaching" (168). This is exactly what the program of *Aeterni Patris* was designed to prevent.

aspects. The first is the result of personal thinking in the new postmodern position, done in the context of the philosophy of history. For it is quite easy to recognize the dated character of Modernist philosophical thinking, and to see that it has been growing intellectually ever more moribund in the years since 1893, 1908, and 1914. This is clear from the viewpoint of God the Father, Creator of heaven and earth, when the discoveries of twentieth century science are recognized and duly considered.[15] It is equally clear from the viewpoint of God the Son, the incarnate Lord of human history, when the philosophy of history is liberated from the Voltairean pattern and allowed to open once again to the prophetic word. And it is not unclear from the viewpoint of God the Holy Spirit, who raises and sustains the Catholic Church as a fact standing in history, quite luminous and visible in the late twentieth century as a great sign in the realm of the human values. In each of the three instances, the philosophy of history is renewed and restored, achieving contact once again with Him who is the Lord of history.

The second aspect of the victory is a social one within the Catholic Church itself. For just as Modernism fastens its grip upon the internal life of the Church chiefly by forcing its ideas in philosophy to prevail in the training of young men for the priesthood, and now also in training for the Ministry of the Word among Religious Sisters and professional religious educators generally, so the victory over Modernism results from postmodern thinking in the design of philosophical curricula, syllabi, and courses of study, thinking which implements the *Optatam totius* of Vatican II.

The key to this is the recognition that the contemporary renewal of philosophy in the Church has been postmodern since its inception in Vatican I and the *Aeterni Patris* of Leo XIII.[16] When the study of

---

[15] See, for example, the recent work of Claude Tresmontant, *Sciences de l'univers et problèmes métaphysiques* (Paris: Seuil, 1976), esp. chap. 1, "A partir de la cosmologie," 11–50, and chap. 3, "A partir de la biologie," 65–111.

[16] If philosophical insight cannot rise to the level of this intellectual perception, there remains obedience to the program of the Holy See from motives linked with the virtue of religion. Those who plan the programs of seminaries and departments of religious education are faced with a decision that is maturing as the twentieth century proceeds: that of turning the mind to Him who is the Lord of history or of preparing the way for another coming of one who serves the Prince of this world, beginning already to genuflect to him. As Pieper observes, the Lord of history and the Prince of this world are quite obviously not the same; see his work, already cited, *Über das Ende der Zeit* (Munich: Kosel-Verlag, 1953), 143. In this connection, Maritain's famous book, *The Peasant of the Garonne: An Old Layman Questions Himself about the Present Time* (New York: Holt, Rinehart, and Winston, 1968), can be studied with profit.

philosophy becomes truly postmodern, candidates for the priesthood and catechists preparing for the Ministry of the Word will study philosophy of the right kind, metaphysically open to objective reality, to the transcendent God of Creation, and to the spirituality of the human soul. And the mode will be that of the philosophy of history, not that of the history of philosophy.[17]

For the older Modernist approach, teaching philosophy as a history of philosophy whereby truth in philosophy is presented naively and simplistically as the result of a timeline emptying into the Modern Age as such, and ending with a "philosophy" that is no longer distinct from the

---

[17] See Battista Mondin, "Philosophy Necessary in Priestly Formation," *L'Osservatore Romano* English Edition (March 2, 1972), 11: "It will not suffice to teach the history of philosophy." The Holy See, in its efforts toward philosophical renewal, always insists that the teaching of philosophy may not be reduced to the presentation of the history of philosophy, merely what others have said and are saying. Students of philosophy themselves personally must be helped to face and to see reality directly. This means a personal grasp of the three basic areas of content: the set of objective and necessary truths proper to philosophical science from which the mind ascends to a personal Absolute and Creator of the Universe and returns from Him to an authentically human concept of man. Cf. *Optatam totius,* §15. For Seminaries, the Holy See desires that philosophy should be studied for two years: cf. the *Ratio fundamentalis* no. 61. Qualitatively, the above threefold minimum division of content should be organized concretely into the studies. And the old-fashioned "history of philosophy" designed to minister to the Modernist mentality should be replaced by a new mode, that of the philosophy of history which helps to reveal to the students the Mystery of Christ, the Lord of history. In a seminary course of four semesters, this can be done readily by devoting the first semester to the birth of Christian philosophy in the catechetical explanations of the First Article of the Creed, in the context of the encounter of the Early Church with the Classical Culture; the second semester to the development of Christian philosophy, with its above-mentioned threefold characteristic content, in the Schools of Christendom; the third semester to the origin, nature, and atheistic bias, due to its immanentism and relativism, of "Modern" philosophy as such; and the fourth semester to the emergence of the postmodern situation in the positive sciences and in philosophy, together with the pastoral reasons for the program of the Church in the teaching of philosophy. This enables young minds to see the efforts of the Holy See toward philosophical renewal in a positive and wholesome light, and not as something marked for subtle sabotage until the Holy See comes at last, as it were, to confess its mistake and to withdraw its many documents on this matter from Vatican I to the present. In the institutes which train catechetical teachers, the same substance of philosophical teaching can readily be given, whether in briefer overview or in a more comprehensive study comparable to that in the Seminaries. The important matter is to treat properly the three basic components of philosophical content, and to do so in the mode of the philosophy of history instead of the history of philosophy. This ministers to *General Catechetical Directory*, no. 88, the breakthrough to "a religious way of thinking" on the part of teachers of the Faith.

positive sciences, will be left behind as outmoded in the postmodern
situation. No longer will young men be forced to go from Kant, Comte,
Hegel, and Marx to the study of theology. On the contrary, when the
design of the syllabus for philosophy and the mode of didactic presentation are properly those of the liberated Christian philosophy of history,
then the relativism and immanentism of Modern philosophy will be
seen in the full context of the construct "Modern," and evaluated from
a superior position in metaphysics, open and free, aware that it is an
autonomous and distinct science with its own proper object and method.

APOSTASY WITHIN

There is a further aspect of Modernism which must be faced if this kind
of philosophical analysis is to be comprehensive in its logic. If Modern
philosophy, as such, in its Cartesian, Spinozan, Kantian, and Hegelian
metaphysics of closure to the God of Revelation, becomes visible as the
fact of a great historical Apostasy from God, then Modernism stands
revealed as the introduction of this same Apostasy inside the Catholic
Church, causing it to course within the arteries by which she lives as an
Institution sent and commissioned to teach the deposit of the Faith.[18]

---

[18] The word "apostasy" was used by *L'Osservatore Romano* (June 29, 1940) in its editorial on the occasion of the death of the unfortunate Father Loisy, when he was termed
"a man who ended in the extremes of negation with regard to all the values of Catholicism, and who therefore has become as it were a symbol on the flag of the most radical
kind of apostasy." This "radical kind" of priestly apostasy can be documented readily
by studying Loisy's work, *La Religion* (Paris: Nourry, 1917), especially in the second
edition (1924) because of its important new preface on mysticism. Henri Bremond
makes a "mystical faith" which dispenses with orthodoxy in the doctrine of the Catholic Faith the basis of his anonymous defense of Loisy: Sylvain Le Blanc, *Un clerc qui n'a
pas trahi: Alfred Loisy d'après ses memoires* (Paris: Nourry, 1931). Forty years later the
author's identity became known and the work has been republished by Emile Poulat,
ed., *Une oeuvre clandestine d'Henri Bremond* (Rome: Edizioni di Storia e de Letteratura, 1972). This *"foi mystique"* has come to pervade Catholic religious education
in some circles as a part of the third moment of the phenomenon after Vatican II.
This shallowly irenic approach which would have and give Jesus Christ without the
Church's formulated doctrine of the Faith which bears Him witness is of course able
to raise up only nominal Catholics. It is this practical bearing upon the life of the
Church which gives acuteness of meaning to the centenary of *Aeterni Patris*. Because
of this new turn into the area of religious education the second century of the philosophical renewal seems destined to be catechetical, where the first century has been
primarily academic.

The implications are immense, and quite obvious: Modernism, true to its nature as Gnosticism reborn, is a betrayal of Jesus Christ, both in general, and in particular as the Divine Teacher of mankind. It represents in contemporary history what can well be termed the ripening Judas phenomenon operating with the priesthood.[19]

This is the special significance of the sacerdotal revolt against the effort of the Church toward philosophical renewal, already noted in connection with the Juvisy Conference in 1933. It was a small fissure at that time, but it continued opening ever wider in the teaching program of the Church as the twentieth century proceeded, until in the years after Vatican II it had reached the proportions of a flood. But this too has its own intelligibility when viewed from the intellectual vantage point of a liberated, postmodern philosophy of history.

A DATED APPROACH

Modernism, to summarize, when subjected to philosophical analysis in the context of the philosophy of history, becomes visible as a dated and historically provincial approach in religious thought. It depends for its very being upon the philosophizing that characterized the Modern Age from Petrarch through Voltaire, Comte and Hegel, Marx and Lenin, to Bergson with his disciple Teilhard de Chardin, and to Nietzsche with his disciple Heidegger. Intellectually it belongs to the nineteenth century. It too ended in the disruptive carnage of the First World War. Its basic intellectual positions were elaborated in its first two phases or

---

[19] See Pius X, *Pascendi* in Vincent A. Yzermans, ed., *All Things in Christ*, 39–90:

> . . . the partisans of error are to be sought not only among the Church's open enemies; but, what is to be most dreaded and deplored, in her very bosom, and are the more mischievous the less they keep in the open. We allude, Venerable Brethren, to many who belong to the Catholic laity, and, what is much more sad, to the ranks of the priesthood itself, who, animated by a false zeal for the Church, lacking the solid safeguards of philosophy and theology, nay more, thoroughly imbued with the poisonous doctrines taught by enemies of the Church, and lost to all sense of modesty, put themselves forward as reformers of the Church; and, forming more boldly into line of attack, assail all that is most sacred in the work of Christ, not sparing even the Person of the Divine Redeemer, whom, with sacrilegious audacity, they degrade to the condition of a simple and ordinary man.

These words apply to all three of the historic moments of Religious Modernism, and not least to the third moment.

moments, indeed in the first one. The current third moment is a light and superficial popularization of those older views, often in more or less secret collusion with the network of cells that props up the intellectual dead horse of Marxism and makes its legs seem to move.[20]

---

[20] Lenin, who always considered himself a *philosophe* in the school of Voltaire, Diderot, and Rousseau, constructed a social machinery or apparatus for holding Modern philosophy over into postmodern times as an ideology, with procedures of thought-control that impose it on minds wherever his Marxist system or empire conquers territory. See Note 91 above; and M.J. LeGuillou, *Le mystere du Père: Foi des Apôtres, Gnoses actuelles* (Paris: Fayard, 1973), 165: ". . . ideology: that is to say, the simple self-justification of an absolute Will-to-Power by means of propaganda. At this point there enters what Nietzsche called 'the struggle for world empire in the name of philosophical ideas'— the époque of ideologies." This is the dark side of the postmodern situation, one that is in the political and social realm, (and in a certain sense also religious—thanks to Religious Modernism). Where social conquest in the name of the ideology is successful, intellectual life must go underground, as it were, where it seems destined to continue in new postmodern ways under the aegis of the Catholic Church. See Oscar Halecki, "The Place of Christendom in the History of Mankind," *Journal of World History* (April, 1954), 948:

> Nothing could be more instructive for the historian to study, if he is interested in the culture of all mankind, than the well-organized distortion of the whole cultural life of all these millions . . . of central and East European peoples, by a foreign imposed totalitarian regime. This is certainly one of the most appalling aspects of the cultural crises of our time. . . . There is indeed a specific Communist interpretation, strictly following the party line, of all sciences, including even biology or philology. But since Marxism is precisely a philosophy of history, based on a method that is supposed to be infallible, and since that interpretation of the past includes a guarantee of Communist victory in the future, no other interpretation can be tolerated and among all scholars the historians are subject to the strictest control under any Communist regime.

Thus the Voltairean philosophy of history is held over into the twentieth century, into postmodern times, and made the ideological basis of an emerging World Empire. But it is an Empire devoid of intellectual and spiritual life. The heart of the matter is in the philosophy of history: intellectual life becomes more and more dependent upon the recognition of the Lord of history. Again Newman is the best guide to further thought and study on these matters, beginning with his Lectures on "The Patristical Idea of Antichrist," in *Discussions and Arguments on Various Subjects* (London: Longman's, 1899), 44–108; see p. 99, where Newman anticipates the aspect of Religious Modernism which has been under discussion here: ". . . an open and blasphemous establishment of infidelity, or some such enormity, in the holiest recesses of the Church." The comment of Edward Holloway in *Catholicism: A New Synthesis* (London: Keyway, 1970), 501, is valid in this connection: "Theological sincerity will rule out most of the 'New Theology' that has been thrust upon us. . . . Much of the counsel offered her [the Church] in even the high places is error, and it is corrosive of her doctrinal truth and continuity with the past. It is also utterly lacking in the realisation of the need for personal prayer, penance, humility, and union with God by meditation and mystical

Victory over this historically dated and philosophically parochial approach in religion results from the advent of postmodern empirical positions in science and postmodern thinking in philosophy, the kind of thinking for which the Church has been calling consistently from Vatican I through Vatican II to the present.

It is a salutary victory. It saves souls. For it preserves in the concluding years of the twentieth century that "religious way of thinking" which is an integral part of persevering loyalty to Him who is the Lord of history.

---

communion. It is hedonist in spirit and very insolent; it is simply a godless 'Humanism' in the vestments of the Church." The postmodern age is one of great intellectual and spiritual liberation, indeed; but not without attention to the coordination of philosophy and theology called for in *Optatam totius*, §14 of Vatican II, a procedure which is ministered in a unique way by the philosophy of history.

9

THE LORD OF HISTORY
AND HIS PAROUSIA

T HE philosophy of history is fundamentally a corollary of the doctrine of Creation, always taught by the metaphysics of Christian
philosophy, and now becoming a postulate of physics and mathematics
as well. Since the Creator is infinitely intelligent, furthermore, philosophical reason by itself can (and should) recognize that He will have a
plan in mind when creating. In carrying out such a plan God is already
the Lord of history. Philosophical reason need feel nothing untoward in
this recognition, nor even in admitting that the plan in itself is beyond
its own scope. For this is nothing more than recognizing creaturehood.

The shame for philosophy is rather in the failure to recognize the
Creator.

PHILOSOPHY AND THE CREED

These insights bring philosophical reason into correlation with the
First Article of the Creed: faith in God the Father Almighty, Creator
of heaven and earth. From this point an attitude of reasonable openness becomes possible to some word from the Supreme Being revealing
the nature of His plan, to the message of the New Testament which
E. Stauffer puts into a brief synthesis: "The *Logos* of the first day, the
Creator's *fiat,* Himself takes on historical form and becomes subject to

successive development, completing in Himself the entire work of creation in its substantive historical reality."[1]

The Catholic Fact, fulfillment of the Hebrew Fact, has been built
into the empirically given of human history by the dynamics of evangelization and catechesis, activities which have proceeded historically in
terms of this same Profession of the Apostolic Faith. For this Profession
goes directly from Creation to the redeeming death of Jesus Christ, His
Resurrection from the dead, and His expected return to judge the living
and the dead.

This *Parousia* is at the heart of the Christian message for it constitutes Him the Lord of history.

Thus God is the Lord of history still, but not in a way humans
would expect or philosophical reason discover. The Lord of history is
the Eternal Son, incarnate—and crucified. He is not the same as the
Prince of this world. He was the Lord of history when, a prisoner with
His hands tied, He was brought before Pilate, who asked Him: "'Are
you the king of the Jews?' Jesus answered . . . 'My kingship is not of this
world.' . . . 'So you are a king?' [said Pilate.] Jesus answered 'You say that
I am a king. For this I was born, and for this I have come into the world,
to bear witness to the truth. Every one who is of the truth hears my
voice'" (Jn 18:33–37).

In enduring the *translatio imperii* which the Great Apostasy will
effect, the Christian philosophy of history will help Christians greatly by
reflecting upon this special character of His Lordship over history. This
Lordship will not be according to the thinking and the ways of men. Thus
the intellectual victory over Religious Modernism, which the philosophy
of history helps to win, is not the same as a social victory for the Church,
a success in this world according to the fallen thinking and desires of men.
To desire this success inordinately for the Church is, in fact, the temp-
tation which lies at the root of the Modernist project to reinterpret the
Christian message, especially the Article of Faith on the *Parousia*.[2]

---

[1] Quoted in J. Danielou, *The Lord of History: Reflections on the Inner Meaning of History*
(London: Longmans, 1958), 191. On Jesus Christ as the center, the origin and the
goal of history, and thus Himself personally the Lord of history, see also the work
of Romano Guardini, *The Lord* (Chicago: Regenery, 1954), esp. "Lord of History,"
439–443, and part seven, "Time and Eternity," 473–571.

[2] See, for example, Father George Tyrrell's "profession of unbelief" in his *Christianity at
the Crossroads* (London: Longmans, Green, 1909), 95:

> The difficulty, for us, lies in the fact that this "idea" [of Jesus] has been trans-
> mitted *too* faithfully in form and not merely in substance; that this apocalyptic

THE CREED AND THE PAROUSIA

Yet the *Parousia,* the Second Coming of Jesus Christ, is of the essence of
the Profession of the Apostolic Faith, and has been since the Apostles
and their writings. It is the characteristic thrust of the entire New Testament and the constant tenor of evangelization and catechesis in the
Early Church as a whole.

"We preach not one coming of Christ," Saint Cyril of Jerusalem
teaches his catechumens,

> but a second as well, far more glorious than the first. The first
> gave us a spectacle of His patience; the second will bring with it
> the crown of the Kingdom of God. . . . Paul indicates these two
> Comings also in writing to Titus in these words: "The grace
> of God our Savior has appeared to all men, instructing us, in
> order that, rejecting ungodliness and worldly lusts, we may live
> temperately and justly and piously in this world; looking for the
> blessed hope and glorious Coming of our great God and Savior
> Jesus Christ" (Titus 2:11–13). Do you see how he speaks of a
> First Coming, for which he gives thanks, and of a second we are
> to look for?

> We find the same lesson in the wording of the Creed we profess,
> as delivered to us, that is, to believe in Him who "ascended into
> heaven and sat down on the right of the Father, and is to come in
> glory to judge living and dead, of whose kingdom there will be no
> end." Our Lord Jesus Christ, therefore, is to come from heaven,
> and to come with glory, at the end of this world, on the last day.

---

imagery has been given a fact-value which our minds have slowly become inca-
pable of accepting. . . . For Jesus, what we call His apocalyptic "imagery" was
no mere imagery but literal fact. But for us it can be so no longer. We can no
longer believe in the little local Heaven above the flat earth, from which Jesus
is to appear in the clouds; nor in all the details of the vision governed by this
conception.

Liberal Protestantism consistently expresses the same negation, just as Reform Judaism
gives up the historic Hebrew faith in a personal Messiah to come in glory. These religious positions represent the old-fashioned quintessence of the "modern," as such. In
the radically altered postmodern universe of intellectual life, there is no problem, for
"above" and "below" relate now to the various wavelengths and impalpable modes in
which it is now understood that even material beings can exist.

For an end of this world there will be; this created world will be made new again. Corruption, theft, adultery and sins of every kind have flooded the earth, and bloodshed has been paid with blood; so to prevent this wondrous dwelling place from continuing forever filled with iniquity, this world is to pass away, to make room for a fairer world. You want proof of this from Scripture? Hearken to Isaiah: "The heavens shall be rolled up like a scroll, and all their hosts shall wither away as the leaf on the vine, or as the fig withers on the fig tree" (Is 34:4). And the Gospel says: "The sun shall be darkened, and the moon will not give her light, and the stars will fall from heaven" (Mt 24:29). Let us not grieve as though we alone were to die, for the stars also will die; but perhaps they will rise again. The Lord shall fold up the heavens, not to destroy them, but to raise them up more beautiful.[3]

THE MYSTERY OF CHRIST

This is no isolated instance, but rather the typical teaching of the Early Church, centered in its characteristic way upon the Mystery of Christ. It is this *mysterium Christi,* "which affects the whole course of human history," that Vatican II in *Optatam totius,* number fourteen, desires philosophy and theology to "supplement one another in revealing to the minds of the students," in a renewed coordination of their distinct intellectual activities.

The philosophy of history, cultivated anew and in its authentic mode, seems to be indicated explicitly as the way to this "more effective coordination."

Mention has been made of the postmodern opportunities for scholarly research and philosophical analysis that are opening before Catholic students. These converge toward the renewal of theology and philosophy and this new kind of coordination between them which illuminates better the Lord of history. The work of research and analysis in the philosophy of history is a special need of the Church, both in academic teaching and in the pastoral and catechetical care of souls, as the

---

[3] Cyril of Jerusalem, *Catechesis XV* in Leo P. McCauley and Anthony A. Stephenson, trans., *The Works of Saint Cyril of Jerusalem* (Washington, DC: The Catholic University of America, 1969), 2:53–55.

twentieth century verges toward its end. Without attempting answers, this study can conclude with a few brief indications regarding typical questions and areas where a new approach, following *Optatam totius,* promises to be fruitful.

There is the question of the basic quality of the interior life proper to the postmodern situation. When she was asked, in the last weeks of her short life on the threshold of the twentieth century, what she meant by her Little Way of confidence in an abandon to the Heavenly Father, St. Therese of Lisieux replied: "It is recognizing one's own nothingness, and looking up to the good God as a little child looks expectantly to his Father."[4] This is the First Article of the Creed and a living of the doctrine of Creation. In her magnificent, lightning-flash intuitions, which put her beyond the Modern Age with its Fathers Renan, Loisy, and the rest, she was postmodern all the way.

Then there is the question of the apostasy, an exercise in the philosophical judgment of values: whether cultural values are truly and authentically human. And the related question whether the present experience is the Great Apostasy of Scripture, or only a more or less distant preparation for it.[5]

Closely related to the apostasy from God is a set of problems relating to the human experience of the *translatio imperii:* deception, discouragement, doubt, misplaced attachments.[6] The analyses made by the

---

[4] In François de l'Immaculée Conception, O.C.D., *Mieux Connaître Sainte Therese de Lisieux* (Paris: Librairie S. Paul, 1955), 32.

[5] John Henry Newman continues to be the best guide on these matters for the English-speaking world. No one knows the day or the hour, for the times are reserved to the Father. But there are also signs of the times, which need the attention of careful Catholic scholarship, especially when a Marxist interpretation of the phrase is gaining headway alongside the Modernist one of "Ongoing Revelation." Cf. R. Guardini, *The* Lord, 467–471: "It is hardly an exaggeration to say that also among Christians profound consciousness of the Lord's return has become a rarity. . . . But does this not entail an essential loss to Christian faith?" (471). In general, the philosophy of history looks to theology for enlightened discussion of the matter; and doubtless both Christian philosophy and sacred theology look forward to a future teaching of the Extraordinary Magisterium on the signs of the times.

[6] Attachments, for example, to the temporal structures of that other Empire of Christian Rome. Catholic Christians ought to be attached to the things of the immortal soul and the lasting home which is to come. See Augustine, *Enarratio in psalmo XCV* (PL 36–37, 1235), commenting on "The world as we know it is passing away" (1 Cor 7:31), and "There is no eternal city for us in this life but we look for one in the life to come" (Heb 13:15). A different kind of attachment, offering a constant challenge to postmodern philosophical analysis throughout the twentieth century, is the bias of Religious Mod-

philosophy of history become increasingly practical, even essential. For example: as the movement against Christ wrests terrain from His sway, space will belong more and more to the Prince of this world. Catholics will be tempted to feel wrong and Religious Modernists, in return for cooperation with the cells of the new Empire, will be made to seem right. Catholics will be tempted to say: "Am I so sure, after all, that I am right? Ought I not to be humble? In fact, do I not sometimes appear even officially to be in the wrong?"

The philosophy of history has a vital role in such a situation, for it changes the fundamental perspective in Christian thinking from space to time, a perspective in which the Prince of this world has only a brief hour. This helps to preserve communion with the Saints of all the Hebrew and Christian times, and loyalty to Him who is the Lord of history.

This historical dimension, ministering to insight and loyalty, is adduced forcefully by Bishop Graber: "If we look back at the Early Church, we can see the old false doctrines of those days reappearing in new garb. Arius, who denied that the *Logos* was of one substance with the Father, lives on. He lives on whenever attempts are made to avoid professing unequivocally that Christ is true God."[7]

---

ernism holding over from the Modern Age even in scholarly works. "Treatises of this type," writes Voegelin, "quite frequently are still indispensable because of their reliable information concerning facts (bibliographical references, critical establishment of texts, etcetera). The damage is rather done through interpretation" (*The New Science of Politics: An Introduction* [Chicago: University of Chicago Press, 1952], 10). Voegelin is writing of the holdover influence of Comtean positivism in certain contemporary treatises on history, sociology, and law, but his insight applies also to work in philosophy and theology. As an example, see Roger Aubert, *Le problème de l'acte de foi*, 4th ed. (Louvain, BE: Nauwelaerts, 1969), where helpful positive scholarship is marred sometimes by insufficient concern for and fidelity to the Church's postmodern program of renewal in philosophy. Aubert's slant becomes visible in his preface to *Progress and Decline in the History of Church Renewal*, Concilium: Theology in the Age of Renewal (New York: Paulist Press, 1967), 27:2: "It is a pity, for example, that we have not been able to find room for . . . the conflict between Catholic intellectuals and *intégristes* (hyperconservatives)." This illustrates well the attitude holding over from the Modern Age: Religious Modernists are "Catholic intellectuals" and those who profess the Apostolic Faith, *quad ubique, quad semper,* and who think philosophically within that same Faith, are "*intégristes* (hyperconservatives)." This is to mistake entirely the meaning of *Aeterni Patris* and the significance of the program for the renewal of Christian philosophy in the contemporary Church. Younger scholars, truly and fully postmodern, are calmly setting aside this kind of obsolete name-calling. *Aeterni Patris* will have its second century.

7   Rudolf Graber, *Athanasius and the Church of Our Time* (London: Van Duren, 1974), 24. The first published work of John Henry Newman, *The Arians of the Fourth*

This loyalty, as a matter of fact, is an outcome of the study of the philosophy of history. It is the link between intellectual life and the Lord of history. It is the practical point where philosophy coordinates with theology in making more manifest, even in the darkness of the other one's brief hour, the splendor of the *mysterium Christi*. It is the founder of Christian philosophy and mankind's greatest philosopher of history who deserves the last word: *Nam qualis amor est Christi, timere ne veniat? Fratres, non erubescimus? Amamus, et timemus, ne veniat. . . . Veniet, velimus nolimus. Non enim quia modo non venit, idea venturus non est.*"[8]

Century (London: Longmans, Green, 1901) continues to be seminal throughout all three moments of the Modernist phenomenon.

[8] Augustine, *Enarratio in psalmo XCV* (PL 36–37, 1235): "What kind of love of Christ is it that fears to have Him come? Brothers, are we not ashamed of ourselves? We love Him and we fear to have Him come! . . . He will come, whether we like it or not. For from the fact that His coming is delayed, it does not follow that He is not going to come."

Epilogue

THE CENTENARY OF
AETERNI PATRIS

THE centenary of the Encyclical *Aeterni Patris* is itself a historical landmark that conveys meaning. Why is this the case? Because it marks a succession of one kind or another in the academic and catechetical orders of teaching in the Catholic Church.[1] But what kind of succession? In answer, one may draw some corollaries of points mentioned in the course of the preceding study. The second century of *Aeterni Patris* appears quite different in present prospect than Pope Leo XIII had hoped, because the reception of his program for the renewal of Christian philosophy in the academic institutions of the Catholic Church has been different than that for which he hoped. Thus *Aeterni Patris* itself, in the vicissitudes of its first century, illustrates a succession in things which ministers to a philosophical understanding of recent Church History.

THE ACADEMIC ORDER

The Holy See was motivated in the program of *Aeterni Patris* by a pastoral concern for Catholic student youth. Through these young people schooled in philosophically renewed academic institutions of the

---

[1] See André Lalande, ed., *Vocabulaire technique et critique de la philosophie* (Paris: Presses Universitaires de France, 1967), 416: "History, third meaning: The very succession of the conditions through which humanity has passed."

Church, the Holy See looked further to a wholesome effect upon the threatened foundations of a now-secularized Christian culture, at home in the West, but spreading its diseased condition to the entire world. *Aeterni Patris,* carrying the teachings of Vatican I into effect, literally had to be done as a part of the pastoral care of souls. For the effects of the philosophical apostasy had already fastened upon the academic order of Western colleges and universities, even the Catholic ones, and had even begun to infiltrate into the seminaries which prepare young men for the Catholic priesthood. This latter fact involves the catechetical order as well, for young men by their very preparation for the priesthood are prepared to be the leaders of the catechetical ministry. Thus the interior life of the Catholic Church was at stake, especially when one considers that the bishops are priests raised to the fullness of the Apostolic Succession and Ministry of the Word. There were therefore concomitant effects of the highest order associated with the primary intention of a pastoral care of Catholic young people in their academic studies.

The Holy See hoped a great hope. By means of the renewal of Christian philosophy, the priesthood and its catechetical order would be protected; and the example and the leadership of Catholic young people restored to their rightful heritage in fundamental thinking would have a salutary effect upon society at large. In fact, Leo XIII in *Aeterni Patris* expresses the hope that academic professors imbued with Modern philosophy would recognize through the ministry of their Catholic colleagues the inherent superiority of this Christian philosophy, with its metaphysical openness to the intelligent Supreme Being, and that the recognition would occasion their recovery of the Catholic Faith itself.

Thus the renewal of Christian philosophy in the academic institutions of the Catholic Church was to become the source of a salutary recovery of intellectual vision and sanity in the apostolate of Western academic life at large. For the People of God, St. Thomas Aquinas writes, has "a science of those things which can be concluded from the Articles of Faith."[2] It is the science of sacred theology, which takes its first principles and point of departure immediately from God through the revelation proposed by His Teaching Church. Hence the human sciences do not judge it. They stand on a lower level, ministering to it as it itself judges them to be helpful. This science proper to the People of God, furthermore, does not identify itself with any culture it encounters in space and time. It is independent, illuminating from above by virtue of those

---

[2] *De veritate,* q. 14, art. 9, ad 3.

first principles, the Articles of Faith, which shine through the entire body of its discourse. And so it is actually one consistent whole with evangelization and catechesis, and is simply that form of the Church's teaching that is scientific in mode.

Christian philosophy is the first academic operation to receive this illumination, because it acts as a guiding star for fundamental thinking. But as more and more young people, holding this source of light personally in hand, take up all the other various arts, sciences, and disciplines of human culture, a wonderful recovery of health through openness to the personal Supreme Being takes place in each of them. Thus the renewed, restored and brightened intelligible light heals and strengthens the values of social life and culture, dependent as they are, as Newman analyzed so well, on the very idea of a university. This light "operates to sublimate them. . . . It permeates them through and through and gives them tone . . . so that we can indeed have a Christian philosophy, a Christian economics and politics, a Christian art, and, more generally, a Christian culture—Christian, that is, in its inner inspiration, and in the way it faces the problems of life in time."[3]

Such was the hope of Pope Pius IX in convening Vatican I. It was the hope of Leo XIII in the program launched by *Aeterni Patris*. It has been the hope of each succeeding Supreme Pontiff to John Paul II in his Constitution *Sapientia Christiana* of April 15, 1979, for the academic order.

Will this Constitution be accepted and implemented in the academic institutions of the Catholic Church? *Sapientia Christiana* stands entirely under the sign of intellectual obedience given out of the virtue of religion. It is the question whether persons of the cloth, they primarily and then the academic laity, are willing to think within the Faith and to administer institutional programs so that they follow it like a

---

[3]   Charles Journet, *The Church of the Word Incarnate* (London: Sheed and Ward, 1955), 1:205–206. One can say that all the Successors of St. Peter in modern times have had this concern, voiced in various ways and in many applications, for the philosophical corrosion which has set upon the fundamental values of Western culture. All these Popes from Pius IX to John Paul II support and illustrate in their documents this word of Pius XI: "Only that is truly and fully human which is Christian, and that which is anti-Christian is inhuman." Cf. John Paul II, Encyclical Letter at the Beginning of His Papal Ministry *Redemptor Hominis*, March 4, 1979. For a pioneering study of the leadership of the Holy See in the rediscovery of the "Historia spiritalis" from Leo XIII through Pius X and Pius XII to the *aggiornamento* of Vatican II, see Pietro Chiochetta, *Teologia e Storiografia della Chiesa: Historia spiritalis* (Rome: Editrice Studium, 1969). This opens up entirely new perspectives for further research that will correlate "philosophy" and "history" in the intellectual life of the Church in the times ahead.

guiding star. As the German historians say, each age stands with its own openness to God, free of compulsion from what has gone before. In the drama of the contemporary renewal of Christian philosophy, everything the Holy See has hoped for in benefit to the academic order and hence to the values of human culture, could take place. Concomitantly, religious education would be healed, secured as authentic catechetics by a priestly ministry shared by many catechetical teachers grounded in their intellectual heritage. The apostolicity of the Catholic Church would thus be projected vigorously intact into the future. Such would be one kind of succession into the second century of *Aeterni Patris*.

On the other hand, the pattern of succession into this coming century of *Aeterni Patris* may project the tacit opposition to the program that was present in certain quarters of Catholic academic life from the beginning and which became a visibly growing phenomenon beginning with the Juvisy Conference in 1933. In such a case, Catholic academic institutions will become increasingly indistinguishable from the secular campuses in full apostasy. Catholic seminaries will increasingly train young men in the ideology of the apostasy. And religious educators will be prepared more and more to administer a pantheistic religious education on behalf of the apostasy.

Thus the agonizing question raised in the Introduction would in such a succession of things become even more acute: If Christ is no longer the center, how can a catechist be Christocentric in teaching? Is not the very Profession of the Apostolic Faith in the Lordship of Jesus at stake?

THE CATECHETICAL ORDER

It is clear that the pattern of refusal of *Aeterni Patris* by Catholic academic institutions as its first century has gone by poses a quite special challenge to the order of catechetical teaching. If the Constitution *Sapientia Christiana* is ignored and disobeyed in the years to come by an academic order dedicated to what is called smoothly "a redimensioning of the Papacy," then the challenge to catechetics will become acute and the danger to the Apostolicity of the Catholic Church will become a menacing reality.

The first thing in such a case is to recognize accurately and lucidly the nature of the situation. By a turn of Providence ever more recognizable as the twentieth century has proceeded, the academic and the catechetical orders of teaching are held separate at the Holy See, with distinct offices located in different sacred congregations. This may well indicate the direction in which accuracy and lucidity are to be found. Catechetical teaching will be called upon to become self-aware, cultivating its own free and independent intellectual life by taking the Articles of Faith as a set of principles and point of departure.

For the Articles of Faith are already the issue. And if the Constitution *Sapientia Christiana* is given the treatment envisaged above as one possibility for the second century of *Aeterni Patris*, then the Articles of Faith will be all that remains to Catholics and to the Catholic Church. The illumination of the values of general cultural life and the temporal order at large will have been snuffed out. Academic institutions generally, whether Catholic or secular, will have become a darkness visible, a darkness ministering to that inhumanity which the Holy See has been foreseeing with pastoral admonition for many decades.

It would be a separate study to trace the concern for "The Deposit of Faith" in the documents of the Holy See that bear upon the philosophical apostasy in the once-Christian Western culture. This concern has been present in these documents ever since 1835. It was so at Vatican I. So too in the documents of Leo XIII on "False Americanism in Religion." John XXIII voiced this concern explicitly when he opened Vatican II. It was the recurring theme of the Pontificate of Pope Paul VI.

Why is the Catholic Church interested in philosophy? Why was there ever such a document as *Aeterni Patris?* Because "The Deposit of Faith" is not a piece of stone dropped from heaven to be carried forward by the Church like an object in a box. It is to be proclaimed from housetops by living heralds and taught by living teachers who explain its Articles of Faith accurately and responsibly. It is carried by the Church in a process of human discourse, the discourse of teaching, a teaching with authority, not like that of merely human philosophers and theologians.

The Catholic Church, in the second century of *Aeterni Patris*, may well concentrate upon the role of Christian philosophy in relationship to this Deposit of Faith. For this is the philosophy which is able to give human ear to the abiding meaning of this same deposit.

Does this mean that catechesis can dispense with academics? Not at all. It means only that the structural framework might be different. If the large and established academic institutions fail to rise to the level of the Constitution *Sapientia Christiana*, then the authentic intellectual life of the Catholic Church will of necessity take place in small units such as St. Philip Neri pioneered and which John Henry Newman chose as the medium best suited to the times he foresaw—and already lived in personally. In such small houses of prayer and study an immensely great intellectual life can indeed be cultivated, one that sees the point of *Aeterni Patris,* one that applies the norms given in *Sapientia Christiana* for the right way to teach philosophy and theology.

Such an intellectual life will carry the Deposit of Faith forward by teaching.[4] It will be ministry to that kind of catechetical teaching which explains the Articles of Faith and helps those who learn them to deepen their conversion to Him whom the Articles of Faith profess. The catechetical order of teaching is thus specifically distinct from all other kinds and disciplines of teaching. By its didactic explanations of them, it communicates the Articles of Faith as such, expressing the Word of God proposed by the authority of the Teaching Church, ever faithful to the same meaning in which this Church of God always has taught them. It is to secure the natural foundations of this meaning that the renewal of Christian philosophy, the natural metaphysics of mankind, will serve in its second century.[5]

---

[4] This is to be a teaching, it is understood, that is on a par from the viewpoint of academic methods with the best teaching in serious universities. See the *General Catechetical Directory,* no. 109. It will cultivate ecclesiastical studies with the same seriousness that physics, for example, still receives in secular universities. This comprehensiveness and seriousness of teaching and learning is a Catholic heritage and it ought to be recovered in ecclesiastical studies: if the academic institutions will not do so, then younger scholars will do so in the newer entities that are already emerging. As a young man, Mozart went from Salzburg to Bologna to study at the small Academy of Music operated by Father Martini, famous for the rigor of his teaching and the comprehensive thoroughness of his examining. This rigor still characterizes the Academies of Music in Italy. The graduates do not regret this, for they know there is no other way to make a musician who is solid. This is what the catechetical order needs, one way or the other.

[5] In other words, the renewal of Christian philosophy was a necessity in its first century for the health and soundness of the academic order. In its coming second century, it will be a necessity for the very existence of evangelization and catechesis, and will be cultivated with perceptive care in the higher institutes of catechetical training. Why? In answer, it may be permitted to cite from the present writer in George A. Kelly, ed., *The Teaching Church in Our Time* (Boston: St. Paul Editions, 1978), 58:

> Because the Creed is neither professed nor explained in the language of one of Karl Rahner's philosophies chosen eclectically, nor one of the theologies emerging from the new pluralism. It is professed in the language of the ordinary man of all times, places and cultures, of fishermen, one may say, who think in the metaphysical constants of natural common sense and express them in the constants of language which linguistic science is able to observe, and which the philosophy preferred by the Church is able to appreciate. This makes the meaning of the Apostolic writings abidingly intelligible without

And what is this meaning? It is nothing else than Jesus Christ, seen in the fullness of His Lordship which the Apostles' Creed professes.

CHRISTOCENTRISM AND THE PHILOSOPHY OF HISTORY

Not least among the benefits of Christian philosophy to evangelization and catechesis is the light it throws upon the simultaneously twofold object of divine faith. Divine faith professes *Ipsa Veritas,* Truth Itself, who is the Supreme Being incarnate now in the fullness of time and able to say in human words: "I am the Truth." Thus God Himself is the direct object of divine faith. But the means whereby the human mind moves toward Him, raises its inner eye to Him, and embraces His goodness with a personal act of its free will is the doctrine which the Catholic Church proposes to mankind in her evangelization and catechesis. This doctrine is the witness of the Church to Jesus Christ. No other witness is available. Peter's question abides: "Lord, to whom shall we go?" Without the witness of this doctrinal teaching, therefore, only Heidegger's brief earthly *Holzweg* remains: a logger's road that fades away, a dusk that turns into night, the nihilism which Nietzsche foresaw and announced.[6]

---

any "New Hermeneutic," and offers the basis for a catechetical communication with men today that is faithful, namely apostolic, in character.

This is perhaps the most fundamental reason for celebrating the centenary of *Aeterni Patris* and for projecting its program forward into the coming times.

[6] It is the tragedy of Modernist priests to concentrate so much upon an ecumenism wrongly understood as to lose their own identity. Cf. note 11, chapter seven, and note 18, chapter eight, on "the shallowly irenic approach" of Father Loisy's non-doctrinal *foi mystique.* Recently a priest well-known in the academic order, giving a paper at Oxford University some months after the constitution *Sapientia Christiana* was promulgated, was heard by the present writer to say that "we are working now to re-dimension the Papacy." Consistent with his light-toned suit and shirt-with-tie outfit, he sought to identify with a concept of ministry which he imagined in his hearers. This anachronism took place in the very times when his hearers not only have taken up the custom of wearing the Roman collar, but are also in a declared search for the authentic Successor of Peter. It is a sign of these times that a young man of his audience protested against his "Chardinian metaphysics" and asked for that original perception of Peter's function that antedates any ecclesiastical use of Greco-Roman juridical concepts and terminology. The renewal of Christian philosophy comes to meet such young men, helping them recognize the sacrificing priests of the New Testament, men endowed with the power to consecrate the Eucharistic elements, a power which no other man possesses, not even baptized and confirmed Roman Catholics.

The Christocentrism to which *Aeterni Patris* and its philosophical renewal minister, as a matter of fact, centers upon the full Jesus Christ of Gospel history, of Eucharistic presence, and of the coming *Parousia*. It ministers to a recovery of the New Testament as a whole, presaged by the fifth weekday preface of the renewed Roman Rite of Vatican II: "With love we celebrate His death; with living faith we proclaim His Resurrection; with unwavering hope we await His return in glory." For the natural thinking which provides the preambles and the foundations for the divine faith of the Catholic Church in the Eucharistic Real Presence of the Risen Jesus Christ is an integral part of the renewal of Christian philosophy. The linearity of the Judeo-Christian view of history is not incompatible with the *exitus-reditus* of St. Thomas' *Summa*, for it bears history forward to this present final stage, to this fullness of time, to this Christian era which is the Eucharistic dawning of the empire of Christ the King which will last forever. [7]

---

[7] Linearity, the movement of a human group from one condition to a succeeding one, is implied by the very concept of fulfillment, the hermeneutic principle used by Christianity in understanding the Hebrew dispensation. Linearity is a fact if the succession of the Testaments is a fact. But this particular linearity is not incompatible with another fact, that this particular succession can be in God's own sense final, in that the Christian Era is, or can be, or at least ought to be, the everlasting effective renewal of the original condition of mankind. This implies something cyclic, like the *exitus-reditus* which is the master concept of St. Thomas' *Summa Theologiae*. If this renewal is not accomplished on this earth, it will be due to the cumulative effect of persons who are deficient causes, failing in lesser or greater degree to make this renewal personally their own. But even so, this world, rendered thus increasingly defective, will serve God well as the temporary scaffolding by which His everlasting structure is built and its living stones are hammered, chiseled, and polished. *Per machinas transituras*, Augustine said with great insight, *domum manentem*—with transitory tools a lasting home is built. Cullmann's book (note 13, chapter one) drew some opposition from those who point out the underlying affinity of the Hebrew worldview with that of the Greeks, the Romans, and indeed all the peoples of the earth, including the great religious traditions of the Orient, all of them aspiring to the renewal of an original justice. But Cullmann's study bears validly upon the concept of history in the cultivated academic life of the classical culture. For a discussion of the point and the literature, see Max Seckler, *Le salut et l'histoire: La pensée de saint Thomas d'Aquin sur la theologie de l'histoire* (Paris: Cerf, 1967), esp. 143–155, "Cycle et linéarité"; an important work translated from the German, *Das Heil in der Geschichte: Geschichtstheologisches Denken bei Thomas von Aquin* (Munich: Kösel Verlag, 1964). These perspectives place Thomas Aquinas in remarkable relationship with all the religious traditions of this planet, validating the title *Doctor Communis* from a new point of view. All of this merits much additional research in the current second century of *Aeterni Patris*, research which will minister to a better appreciation of the significance of the Real Presence of Jesus Christ in the Eucharist. There has been a tendency in the Christian Era not only to reject the doc-

The kind of thinking on the meaning and direction of universal history which this present study exemplifies can of course hardly please those whom Maritain has rather incisively termed the ideosophists of the Modernist movement. The Catholic intellectual life of the second century of *Aeterni Patris* will be called upon to exercise great forbearance toward them, for not a few will be fellow priests, "peace-priests," as it were, who will think to accommodate with an outwardly triumphant Marxism. A situation is developing which calls for forbearance, patience, and much fraternal dialogue with them designed to help them see that their shallow kind of ecumenism obstructs that true ecumenism which already professes the Apostles' Creed and which is gradually discovering the Victim for sin, the Lamb of God really present and offered daily in the Sacrifice of the New Testament.

But there will always be not a few priests and religious who already give a hearing to this kind of thinking about the wonderful works of God "from Genesis to the present times of the Church." Already the younger ones are at hand. They recognize in the Christian philosophy of history the perspective of Newman, Aquinas, and Augustine, the perspective proper to those who wish to abide in communion with the Church of the Apostles.

With such priests and religious there will be the immense body of the Catholic laity, raising their families and deeply concerned for the eternal salvation of their children.[8] For all such persons, Christo-

---

trine of the Real Presence, but also among Catholics to undervalue or even in practice to overlook the fact of this Presence. This has been the case strangely enough even in religious houses, as the revelations to St. Margaret Mary bear witness. In the second century of *Aeterni Patris* it can be expected that the original thought of the Fathers of the Church regarding the Eucharist will be seen more comprehensively and accurately. See the pioneering study of Raymond Johanny, *L'Eucharistie centre de l'histoire du salut chez Saint Ambroise de Milan* (Paris: Beauchesne, 1968).

8   For a remarkable and timely example of a layperson's insight regarding the relationship of St. Thomas Aquinas to the essential truths and values, see the work of the well-known French laywoman Renée Casin, *Saint Thomas d'Aquin ou l'Intelligence de la Foi* (Montsûrs, FR: Editions Resiac, 1973). France continues to be the eldest daughter of the Church, experiencing things first. The laity have made this work available in an English translation by Dr. James Likoudis: Renée Casin, *Saint Thomas Aquinas, Orthodoxy, and Neo-Modernism in the Church* (New Rochelle, NY: Catholics United for the Faith, 1977). With keen insight the author has taken for the structure of her book the four signs of recognition stated by the Catholic laity left by the interrupted mission of St. Francis Xavier in Japan; if the reception of the constitution *Sapientia Christiana* in the academic institutions of the Catholic Church proves to be negative in the second century of *Aeterni Patris,* the resulting deception may bring the laity

centrism is of the essence. For them, Peter's question abides: "Lord, to whom shall we go?"

These Catholic priests, religious, and laity of the second century of *Aeterni Patris* will have some questions of their own which involve the philosophy of history. For example: Are they who look upon themselves as Catholics, indeed, but updated and "Chardinian," not benighted and obscurantist like these others, not perhaps going toward someone other than Jesus Christ? Preparing his way? Announcing his coming? *Nuntii eius*, in Aquinas' perceptive phrase? But this coming one, who will he be? What good will he do? What lies beyond his deceptive promises? Will he raise anyone up on the last day? Is it not better to be faithful to the Lord of history?

The particular moment of the centenary of *Aeterni Patris* brings such questions to mind. They imply the Christocentric answer to which the Christian philosophy of history points, the answer which begets confidence for the coming second century of the program of Vatican I, Vatican II, and the Holy See on behalf of the natural metaphysics of mankind. For these questions call for the program which helps "reveal to minds . . . with ever increasing clarity the Mystery of Christ, which affects the whole course of human history, exercises unceasing influence on the Church, and operates mainly through the ministry of the priest."[9]

---

elsewhere to give them heed. For Renée Casin's use of these hallmarks, see pp. 30–31 of the English translation:

> These were the four touchstones of the Faith appealed to by the forgotten Christians of Nagasaki who once again encountered Catholic missionaries after an interruption of three centuries. Yes, for three centuries these Japanese Christians had lived heroically without any priests, with no sacraments other than baptism and marriage, without churches and without books, as well as being continually harassed and wounded by the Imperial police. It was one of their spokesmen who joyfully reminded the astonished Père Petitjean: "Our fathers have taught us what they held from their fathers: You will recognize the ministers of the true God by this four-fold sign of purity: the Eucharist, the Virgin, the White Father of Rome, and the celibacy of the priests. . . ." And since we have discovered in St. Thomas a champion of truth and intelligence, he will now aid us to find again those four essential truths of the Faith which serve as the true test of Catholicity: the Eucharist, the Priesthood, the Papacy, and the Blessed Virgin Mary. Each of these Catholic dogmas has been utterly devalued by those who have lost at the same time their understanding of the faith and the sense of sin.

[9] Paul VI, Decree on the Training of Priests *Optatam totius*, October 28, 1965, §14, in Austin Flannery, O.P., ed., *Vatican Council II: The Conciliar and Post Conciliar Documents* (New York: Costello, 1975), 717–718.

Index